Diana R. Boggia, MEd

# Parenting
## *with a* Purpose

### Inspiring, Positive Alternatives to Reach and Teach Your Child How to Behave

iUniverse, Inc.
Bloomington

**Parenting with a Purpose**

*Inspiring, Positive Alternatives to Reach and Teach Your Child How to Behave*

*iUniverse books may be ordered through booksellers or by contacting:*

*iUniverse*
*1663 Liberty Drive*
*Bloomington, IN 47403*
*www.iuniverse.com*
*1-800-Authors (1-800-288-4677)*

*Because of the dynamic nature of the Internet, any web addresses or links contained in this book may have changed since publication and may no longer be valid. The views expressed in this work are solely those of the author and do not necessarily reflect the views of the publisher, and the publisher hereby disclaims any responsibility for them.*

*Any people depicted in stock imagery provided by Thinkstock are models, and such images are being used for illustrative purposes only.*

*Certain stock imagery © Thinkstock.*

*ISBN: 978-1-4759-1542-6 (sc)*
*ISBN: 978-1-4759-1543-3 (hc)*
*ISBN: 978-1-4759-1544-0 (e)*

*Library of Congress Control Number: 2012907259*

*Printed in the United States of America*

*iUniverse rev. date: 5/23/2012*

# Endorsements

As a pediatrician, I have seen the good, the bad, and, unfortunately, the ugly regarding parenting techniques and child behavior. I have also seen firsthand the successful results of Diana's techniques in my patients. In *Parenting with a Purpose*, Diana provides parents with a workable blueprint to help them develop well-behaved, confident children who would make any parent proud. I highly recommend this collection as a valuable parenting resource.

*Dr. Larry Hardwork, Akron Children's Hospital*

As a mother of two young children, I have found the information in *Parenting with a Purpose* to be easy to read, easy to apply, straightforward, hands-on, and seasoned with personal experience and humor. Whenever I have a question, I know I can find a simple, effective answer within these pages. I love it!

*Tricia Dever, former special education teacher*
*and mother of two under four*

Diana Boggia has compiled a parenting gem! She offers clear information, valuable resources, and honest opinions on topics ranging from potty training through handling the holidays to dealing with bullying. Her working knowledge of child development and family issues, coupled with her personal parenting experience, makes her writing simultaneously authoritative and warmly supportive. In addition, despite tackling difficult or painful issues, she is solution focused and optimistic about what parents can accomplish with love and consistency. This book is truly a valuable resource for any parent.

*Bobbi L. Beale, PsyD, clinical psychologist*

Raising a toddler has been the hardest thing I've ever done. I'll take covering a hurricane over battling with a two-year-old any day. I'm physically and emotionally worn out every night, so finding time to read a book on parenting is a luxury. Worse yet, every book I pick up for advice is too wordy and complicated and, frankly, not all that helpful. Every book, that is, until this one. Finally, here is an easy-to-read book with great, simple advice. I marvel that the seemingly tiny changes that Boggia recommends have made life with my little ones so much better for us all. Instead of yelling, I spend my days laughing with my well-behaved kids. How wonderful is that!

*Melinda Murphy, former CBS Television newscaster*
*and now mother of two under three*

Diana provides useful and practical information that produce positive results. She writes about a nurturing, positive approach that includes making gentle physical contact to gain a child's attention prior to attempting behavior remediation. Her suggestions help parents feel more capable in their interactions with their children. This empowerment can lead to an improved parent/child relationship, improved communication, and a reduction of acting-out behaviors. Diana also includes her personal experiences as a single parent raising her three children, which helps readers know that she has "walked the walk." Her personal disclosures, coupled with her formal graduate training, make *Parenting with a Purpose* a must-read for all those with children.

*Randi Motz, MA, MEd, LPCC-S*

Diana's insight and wisdom on the issues that parents face today is a tremendous resource. Grandparents, buy this book and give it to your children. It works!

*Dick and Judy Hickman, grandparents*

The information within each chapter can easily be used as a guide to spark conversation and provide direction for a weekly mom's support group.

*Danette Lund, MEd, director of programs and services,*
*Early Childhood Resource Center*

*Parenting with a Purpose* is a well-organized compilation of parenting advice in a clear, concise format that is easy to read and follow. Diana's gift of writing not only gives the reader sound child development techniques but also provides her own personal experiences in this practical parenting handbook. I highly recommend this book to both parents and teachers.

*Suzanne Griffiths, forty-two years in the field of early childhood as a speaker, trainer, and nursery school director*

I love it! I have seen firsthand how Diana's positive strategies improve children's behaviors and impact an entire family. She facilitated parenting groups for Valley Pediatrics for more than eight years, helping many parents address and remediate their behavioral concerns. I continue to refer families to her whenever they are looking for answers, and now, I can also tell them to buy the book!

*Dr. Irene Shevelev, pediatrician*

I dedicate this book to my three children, Benjamin, Matthew, and Eliza, who uncovered my well of deep, unconditional love. They provided the foundation for the research, practice, and perfection of positive parenting and have grown to be wonderfully successful adults I am so proud of. Stories from their childhood years are captured throughout many pages within this book, as I felt it important to share the struggles, joys, and strategies that built their successes.

To my parents, Bonnie and David, I thank you for the way in which you raised me, the strong values you instilled, and the love and support you have always given. My childhood memories are filled with magic and comfort, both of which are described within these pages.

To my amazing husband and best friend, Robert Mayone, your endless efforts, patience, encouragement, and support have resulted in this book, which was once only a dream.

As I say, "Once you become a mother, you no longer live life for yourself because, once you become a mother, everything changes. Schedules change. Relationships change. The things that were once important change. Life is changed forever. I believe that life has been changed for good."

# Contents

# Introduction

This book is a selection of published articles from my weekly syndicated newspaper column, *Family Matters*. The positive approach throughout each article will nurture and enhance appropriate, thoughtful behavior, as well as provide positive alternatives to help parents minimize or eliminate misbehaviors. More detailed information is found in *Parenting with a Purpose* than was originally printed, as articles were edited for newspaper publication. Each page addresses a specific behavior or parental concern and has been categorized for easy reading. At the close of each chapter, you will find "Dear Diana" questions from parents who have asked for suggestions or direction. You will find strategies to remediate misbehaviors, increase self-confidence, and empower yourself as a parent as you learn to take control in a positive way, without yelling or harsh punishment.

Throughout *Parenting with a Purpose*, information is provided regarding your child's development: what he hears and how he thinks.[1] Although the child development chapter includes only birth through five years, the positive approach throughout these pages is effective with toddlers through teens. Hundreds of strategies are provided throughout to improve behavior and nurture your child's spirit by what you do, how you do it, what you say, and how you say it. Imagine being completely confident in managing your child's behavior, whether you are out in public or at home. Read how to empower yourself and retrain your child with positive interventions to eliminate confrontations. Read how to de-escalate temper tantrums, soothe your child to sleep, or implement a time-out with success, not anger. Read how to teach your child to wait patiently while you are on the phone, to pick up after himself, to develop thoughtful manners, and to develop a strong sibling bond, all accomplished while building independence and self-confidence. Learn to communicate so

---

1   I have used the masculine pronoun throughout, but it is only for efficiency purposes. Not only is this material for both sexes, it is also for, at times, all ages.

that your child can understand exactly what you are asking of him. Read about the effectiveness of multisensory communication, which can change the dynamics of your entire family. These pages clearly and simply explain how each strategy can be easily and successfully implemented with your child in your home.

As a single mother of three, I made it my mission to parent with a purpose, ensuring resiliency by instilling self-confidence and building critical life skills. The strategies, implementation, educational material, and suggestions within are parent proven and written based upon nearly thirty years of working with families, my personal experience, years of training in child development, and the professional opinions obtained from those in the fields of medicine and child psychology.

No matter what parenting style you are comfortable with, you can easily incorporate the small changes that will make all the difference in your child's life. Embrace parenting with passion and joy. Meet your child's insatiable quest for love and learning with tenderness and thoughtful teaching. Anyone can be a parent, but it takes a parent armed with skills and continuous dedication to raise a resilient, thoughtful, self-confident child. The strategies within these pages are simple, but the results are absolutely remarkable. You will see a difference within days.

*Tell me, and I'll forget. Teach me, and I'll remember. Involve me ...*
*and I'll learn.*

Benjamin Franklin

# Words of Encouragement

At one time or another, all parents have experienced some sort of difficulty or felt disappointment, humiliation, or embarrassment with their child's behavior. All parents have also felt joy and deep pride with their child's successes and achievements. The following are thoughts and words of encouragement from those who believe in *Parenting with a Purpose*:

"If you bungle raising your children, I don't think whatever else you do well matters very much."

*Jacqueline Kennedy Onassis*

"A child educated only at school is an uneducated child."

*George Santayana*

"You can learn many things from children. How much patience you have, for instance."

*Franklin P. Jones*

"Children require guidance and sympathy far more than instruction."

*Ann Sullivan*

"A child knows that she is always safe in her mother's arms. Mothers lift up their child not only with their arms, but also with their hearts, whenever they need lifting."

*Diana Boggia*

"Where did we ever get the crazy idea that, in order to make children do better, first we have to make them feel worse? Think of the last time you felt humiliated or treated unfairly. Did you feel like cooperating or doing better?"

*Jane Nelson*

"Children have never been very good at listening to their elders, but they have never failed to imitate them."

*James Baldwin*

"When I approach a child, he inspires in me two sentiments: tenderness for what he is and respect for what he may become."

*Louis Pasteur*

"We worry about what a child will become tomorrow, yet we forget that he is someone today."

*Stacia Tauscher*

"Look at the world through the eyes of your child. Show him the beauty in each day. Teach him with patience and kindness. Love him with all your heart."

*Diana Boggia*

"When I was a boy of fourteen, my father was so ignorant I could hardly stand to have the old man around. But when I got to be twenty-one, I was astonished at how much the old man had learned in seven years."

*Mark Twain*

"Bitter are the tears of a child: Sweeten them. Deep are the thoughts of a child: Quiet them. Sharp is the grief of a child: Take it from him. Soft is the heart of a child: Do not harden it."

*Pamela Glenconner*

"Children are our most valuable natural resource."

*Herbert Hoover*

"Making the decision to have a child—it's momentous. It is to decide forever to have your heart go walking outside your body."

*Elizabeth Stone*

"There are only two lasting bequests we can hope to give our children. One is roots; the other, wings."

*Hodding Carter*

# Parenting Styles and Strategies

## Introduction to Parenting: What's Your Style?

Parenting styles vary from family to family and parent to parent. Some parenting styles are cultural. Many of us parent as our parents did, while others vow to never parent as their parents did. How we were parented taught us how to respond, how to behave, and what was expected of us. We carry those experiences with us, which is important to remember as you now parent your own young child.

Some parents laugh from embarrassment when their child misbehaves. Some parents ignore misbehaviors, perhaps because they don't want to escalate the situation or don't know how to address the situation properly. Some parents react to misbehaviors by yelling or spanking, only to later regret their actions and apologize. Some rule with an iron fist, while others don't provide rules at all. Specific components to successful parenting provide the scaffolding for the development of a successful child.

Parents who seek exposure to continuous teaching opportunities are successful in providing the experiences that help build positive self-esteem, effective communication, acceptable social skills, and successful independence. Parents who recognize a temper tantrum as an opportunity to teach appropriate behaviors are more successful in minimizing tantrums overall and will experience fewer public displays. Those parents who set their children up for success by communicating their expectations, rather than simply expecting their children to behave, will get better results. So many methods can improve a child's behavior, but simply expecting him to behave won't produce the behavior you desire. Children need to be taught repeatedly, by example, with multisensory communication, consistency, and love. I have provided positive strategies throughout this chapter to help you set your child up for success by nurturing desired behaviors and reinforcing them with your focused attention.

Most children learn what they live. They watch everything we do and listen closely to all we say. Be aware of what you expose your child to. Once he has seen or heard it, it will be part of his life experience. Protect your child, and teach with love, not impulsive reactions. Teach with consistency, providing the same answer, so your child can learn what to expect from you and understand what is expected of him. Teach outside the event, after you have had an opportunity to think carefully about the best way to help your child learn.

This chapter provides information, along with interventions with a positive approach, in response to specific questions or situations brought up by parents looking for alternatives to redirect, reframe, or remediate their child's behavior. You can teach or retrain your child by providing the information in a variety of ways, including direct communication and modeling. Raising a child requires unconditional love, consistency, a watchful eye, thoughtful teaching, a listening ear, and an open heart. Any behavior can be changed, just as any child can be taught the skills you want him to have. The determining factor is how you teach them. You are your child's teacher of life for the rest of his life.

Parent with a purpose, providing your child with everything he needs, because it is just not quite good enough to parent with love alone.

## Children Learn What They Live

It is not easy to be a parent. Children test limits throughout the day, every day, because that is how they learn. Parents set boundaries. They push the limit. Then parents set boundaries again. Those with more than one child know the frustration and chaos that can occur when trying to correct or redirect one child, only to have a sibling come around to stir the pot, tease, or deliberately attempt to escalate the situation. They yell, and parents yell at them to be quiet. They hit a sibling, and parents spank or slap their wrist while screaming, "Don't hit!" Children can be embarrassingly loud at home, throughout the neighborhood, and in public, totally unaware that they are affecting everyone around them. They learn by what is modeled for them, so be mindful of what you are teaching your observant learner.

Years ago, I was given a refrigerator magnet that says, "Parenting is the toughest job you'll ever love." I found that to be so true. I loved raising my children, and I love being a mom. I gave it my all. My three children lived through my parenting mistakes and learned much as they were growing up. There was a long, difficult divorce, and too often they were caught in the middle. We faced unbelievable challenges, and on some days it was difficult to get up in the morning to begin another day. There were tears, but there was always laughter. There were arguments, but there were always hugs. There was hurt, but there was always an abundance of love.

I often speak with parents who ask, "Why does my child act the way he does?"

I respectfully answer, "You are his role model, and he is learning you." When a parent stands in disbelief, I rephrase and say, "If not here and from you, then where?"

I love the phrase "more is caught than taught," meaning that children carefully watch everything we do and learn directly from our example. Of course, many influential people are in a child's life—friends, teachers, and family—who directly impact your child as he learns by watching and listening. However, the foundation of who they truly are and how they navigate through life comes from how they live from the boundaries you provide and the unconditional love you show consistently every day. I'm sure you will recognize the familiar verse below, but take a minute to read Dorothy Law Nolte's words:

If a child lives with criticism, he learns to condemn.

If a child lives with hostility, he learns to fight.

If a child lives with fear, he learns to be apprehensive.

If a child lives with pity, he learns to feel sorry for himself.

If a child lives with ridicule, he learns to be shy.

If a child lives with jealousy, he learns what envy is.

If a child lives with shame, he learns to feel guilty.

If a child lives with encouragement, he learns to be confident.

If a child lives with tolerance, he learns to be patient.

If a child lives with praise, he learns to appreciate.

If a child lives with acceptance, he learns to love.

If a child lives with approval, he learns to like himself.

If a child lives with recognition, he learns that it is good to have a goal.

If a child lives with sharing, he learns about generosity.
If a child lives with honesty and fairness, he
learns what truth and justice are.
If a child lives with security, he learns to have
faith in himself and in those about him.
If a child lives with security, he learns that the
world is a nice place in which to live.
If you live with serenity, your child will have peace of mind.
With what is your child living?[2]

When your child is respectful, honest, confident, perseverant, hardworking, generous, kind, tender, empathetic, thoughtful, loving, and patient, take a minute to think about how he developed those wonderful attributes and who taught him. Then say to yourself, "He must have been watching."

## Seven Steps to Effective Parenting

The way in which you communicate to your child will determine how clearly your message will be received. The consistency with which you teach will determine how well your child will learn. Providing rules and guidelines, with incentives and consequences, will teach your child what to expect and what is expected of him. Johanna Miller, psychological assessor at Child and Adolescent Behavioral Health in Canton, Ohio, provided some of the following information to improve behaviors:

1.  Provide simple, clear instructions. Many parents talk too much. The more they talk, the less children hear. Give clear, simple instructions and explanations for tasks throughout the day. If a task is complex or lengthy, break it down into more manageable steps.

2.  Determine family rules. Create a list of family rules and expectations for behavior, and post them in a prominent location. Involving your child in the process will encourage him to take more responsibility for his choices and behaviors.

---

2   J. Canfield and H. C. Wells, *100 Ways to Enhance Self-Concept in the Classroom: A Handbook for Teachers and Parents* (Boston: Allyn & Bacon, 1976).

3. Increase compliance by increasing positive reinforcement of desired behaviors. Catch your child being good. Whenever your child follows a direction or command, no matter how small, praise or recognize that behavior. For example, you could say, "I see you made your bed this morning," or "I noticed you hung up your jacket by the door." Practice compliance by giving your child several simple "when and then" commands within a short period of time, such as, "When your show is over, then it's time to turn off the TV." Provide recognition when the command is followed.

4. Pay attention to how you give commands. Make sure you really mean it. It sounds obvious, but many frustrated parents give command after command, hoping a child will follow one of them. Never ask a child to do something. Tell him to do it. Don't say, "Try to be home on time." Instead, say, "Be home by five." Keep commands simple. The more words a parent uses, the less a child will hear. Break complex tasks into several steps, and praise your child after he completes each step before providing the next. Finally, make sure you have your child's attention. Stand in front of him, touch him gently, get down to his level, provide the directive, and then have him retell you what he is to do. This is called "reflective listening."

5. Create positive rewards. Work with your child to set up a reward system for expected everyday tasks, including completing homework without complaints or getting ready for bed without grumbling. Chores, such as cleaning the bathroom or helping around the house, need to be assigned, reinforced, and rewarded upon completion. Behavior goals, such as listening the first time, sharing, speaking rather than screaming, and so forth, can change how your child functions when you have a specific idea of the behavior you want. Use tokens, stickers, or points to help your child visually track what he has earned. These can be displayed on a chart with stickers, kept in a clear jar using tokens, or listed in a "bank book" with points. Create a list of rewards with your child to work toward, for example, five tokens equals one hour of extra TV, two stickers equals one half hour of a video game, fifteen points equals a movie rental, and so forth. The rewards should be given in addition to ongoing parental praise, and of course, hugs are always free. Adolescents may act as if a hug is the last thing

they desire, but everyone actually loves a hug. Children often tire quickly of rewards, so be sure to frequently change the type of reward your child can earn.

6. Choose appropriate, natural consequences for poor behavior. When your child is misbehaving, make every effort to maintain a calm, controlled demeanor. Keep your voice level and firm. Do not scream, threaten, or spank. Restate your expectation. If, after trying to understand why your child has misbehaved, you determine that the offense needs a consequence, make it a natural one. "Since you refused to turn off the TV when I told you to, you have lost the privilege of watching any more TV for the rest of the day."

7. Always set a good example for your child. Children need role models to learn appropriate behavior, and the adults in their lives are critically important. Give yourself a break if you realize that, due to your anger or frustration, you are making a conflict worse, not better. Say, "I'm very angry right now. Go to your room. I will speak with you about this in ten minutes." This is a great way to model for your child how to take time out to regain self-control. Children learn what they live. As a parent, you can show, do, and say what you want your child to know and to grow to be.

## Teach Rather Than Negotiate

Do you repeat yourself or feel frustrated or worn out trying to get your child to listen the first time? Does your child ignore what you say or incessantly negotiate until you give in? Some parents are accepting of those negotiations and label their child as "strong-willed." I have heard parents speak right in front of their child, saying, "He's just so strong-willed that I don't know what to do!" Unfortunately, with that one statement, they have just empowered their child.

Providing clear directives and following through with consistency can be two of the most difficult actions a parent must take. Following through with consistency is also one of the most wonderful gifts a parent can give to a child. Children raised with structure, boundaries, consistency, fairness, and unconditional love will grow up to be successful within the guidelines of life. It is often exhausting to stay the course, not being swayed by begging, pleas, argument, negotiation, objections, and challenges. Parents need to be reminded not to take it personally when they hear, "You are the meanest mom ever!" or "I wish I had a different mother." Succumbing to parental uncertainty in decision making sends a direct message to a child that he can push and pressure until his parent changes his mind. Parental indecision actually teaches a child how to manipulate, misbehave, and negotiate, even at a young age. A common example is when a child asks for candy at the checkout, and his parents say, "No, not today." Typically, that child will whine, and his parent will say, "No, don't ask me again." Next, the child will cry, and the parent will say, "I'm getting angry. I said no. Stop crying." When that child has escalated to a full-blown temper tantrum, the parent tosses the candy to the child out of anger and defeat to minimize embarrassment and to stop the screaming. Unfortunately, at that moment, that parent has just trained his child to yell louder and longer each time because he has learned that his parent will eventually give in. A child will gradually become empowered each time his parent gives in. Children learn by testing limits. Think of it as their job to continually push and to test to see if the rules have changed. They learn social and interpersonal skills as well as cause and effect as they navigate through each day. How we respond to them will determine how they respond to us and others throughout their lives. The next time you are in the candy aisle and your answer is no, stay strong, and do not change your mind under pressure.

## Some Tips to Stay Strong

- **Think it through.** Think about your child's question before you say no. When your child asks for something, a first response is often no, without even really thinking it through. If the answer is no, then be prepared to stick with your decision. You will undoubtedly get pushback, crying, yelling, or even a full-blown tantrum until your child learns that you do not change your mind any more.

- **Take your time to answer.** The best response is given when you are calm and you can make a decision based upon your child's best interest. Do not make a decision only to change your mind later. A successful response is, "I will think about it and let you know before dinner." Provide a time limit on your answer. If your child pushes or insists on an answer, let him know that, if he continues to ask, the answer will be no. However, if he is able to wait for an answer, you will give it some thought. This can be difficult to implement while emotions are running high. Practice using the phrase, "I'll give it some thought." Your child will learn patience and learn to accept your response.

- **Don't defend.** It is a good decision, and you are certain about it. There is no need to justify, defend, or explain your reasoning. Do not feel pressured into answering, and do not lose your temper or yell. Yelling, negotiating, or defending can often escalate a situation; when you defend, you're done! When parents explain too much by defending an answer, it can become an invitation to a debate because they have opened the door for negotiation.

- **Offer options and distractions.** For a two- to four-year-old who wants what he wants when he wants it, tell him when he can rather than why he can't. Distract him with an item to look at or hold. Take him by the hand and physically remove him to a new setting. Engage him in a new or different activity. If you bend, you will be training your child to beg. Inconsistency can extend the length of a tantrum each time he wants something.

- **Become a parent-in-training.** Rather than dread those temper tantrums, embrace them! Consider yourself a parent-in-training. Use every opportunity to practice, stay strong, and face a tantrum. When you dread a tantrum, your child will sense it and take advantage. When you are ready, you will feel strong, and you will know you are providing the right limits. Your child will sense your empowerment. Use every opportunity and every tantrum to implement your new skills and training tactics.

- **Provide empathy with indifference.** Tell your child you understand that he is disappointed and you are very sorry he is upset over your decision. Repeat when he will be able to do whatever he requested. Reach out to make that connective touch. Remain consistent by using the same words each time.

Teach your child that he can rely on you. When you say yes, do not go back on your word. Before you say no, think it through and then stick to it.

## A Positive Role Model

Take a survey. Ask yourself if your child is resistant to your requests or directives. Do you feel as if your child is controlling the house? Is he saying or doing inappropriate things? Without realizing it, you may be training him to behave that way. Most of us would respond, "Absolutely not!" However, parents often say and do things that send mixed messages, actually teaching a child to become oppositional, resistant, and rude. Sometimes when a parent says "no," the child hears "maybe." When a parent says "don't," the child immediately does. Young children naturally respond this way to learn about boundaries and to gain a sense of how the parent will respond or what the parent will tolerate. A parent's response teaches a child how to behave, and he is likely to behave in the same manner each time after that once he has been taught.

I observed a mother every day as she dropped off her son for therapy. She always said, "Give me a hug good-bye." From the very first day, her child responded, "No! I don't want to!" Using what she referred to as child psychology, she said, "Okay, never mind. I don't want a hug anyway." As she walked away, her son came running for a hug every day. I watched as the teaching continued each morning, observing this little boy developing his routine of refusal (to comply with hugs) until his mom said she didn't want hugs. What began as a game had evolved into giving her son complete control each morning. She taught and reinforced his resistance until he was ready to change his mind. Each time she hugged her child in this situation, she reinforced his defiant behavior. I continued to work with him regularly, and he continued to be oppositional throughout the day because it had become an effective response for him. He was in control.

Young children are concrete learners. They cannot decipher innuendoes, implications, or sarcasm. They process statements literally until they develop more abstract thinking in preteen years.

I have seen many parents laugh when their toddler has dropped something and then used profanity on cue. Laughter will reinforce a behavior, even if a parent says, "Don't say that," while laughing. It is a confusing message for a child. Eventually, a child will be admonished or punished for using the exact same language for which he previously received laughter and reinforcement. Whether a parent laughs out of embarrassment or because he thought an inappropriate behavior was cute, a child learns through trial and error and will continue to do whatever is reinforced.

A father once asked for my help because his seven-year-old daughter was cursing at him, gesturing with her finger when she was upset. I explained to her that the words and gesture she used were rude, inappropriate, and ugly. I asked where she learned it, and she looked over toward her dad, who admitted he was to blame. She had learned it all from him. He was determined to change his behavior and to be a better role model. She agreed to communicate when she became upset by talking to her dad rather than screaming at him. Children repeat what they hear and do what they see.

I have seen parents who yell at their children and then pull them up on their lap while explaining what they did wrong. It is confusing for a child to be admonished and then cuddled for an inappropriate behavior. It is much better to bend down to your child's level, clearly communicating what is and is not allowed. Some parents may think that inappropriate toddler behaviors are funny or cute and will say, "Oh, you're so bad," as they laugh, hug, or tickle their child. Again, that mixed message is confusing to a young child in training. What may be a cute behavior in a three-year-old is usually not cute behavior in a five-year-old and is obnoxious in a teenager.

Sometimes parents bribe their children to get them to comply. The definition of bribery is to provide a gift to corrupt or change a behavior. Bribery empowers a child, allowing him to decide if the reward (the bribe) is great enough. Children who are bribed quickly learn that they are in control and don't have to comply unless a gift or prize is offered. Parents will confuse their child when they consistently bribe but become angry and refuse to bribe or give in one day. A child cannot adjust because the rules have changed. Children learn best when their parents model the behavior they want. Be clear, be kind, and be consistent.

## Communication, Consequences, and Consistency

Some parents may actually challenge their child to do the opposite of what they want without even realizing it.

A child says, "No, I don't want to."

A parent replies, "Well, that's fine. I don't want you to do that anyway."

The parent empowers the child as well as teaches him to defy. Bribes and threats also are ineffective, as they empower a child to choose a reward when bribed or say "I don't care" when threatened.

## Making Changes

There are three important components to teaching or retraining a child. You can decrease defiance and improve overall behaviors by providing clear communication, recognition of positive behaviors, and appropriate consequences. An overall attitudinal change from defiance to compliance may take time, but it will happen. Small, positive behavioral changes will be noticeable within days. Setbacks are normal, so be prepared for them. When you remain calm and consistent, you will absolutely achieve the results you are looking for.

## Clear Communication

Present your directives in a kind voice in three sentences or fewer:

1. It's time to (do your homework).

2. Let me know if you need any help.

3. When you're finished with your homework, then you may (play outside, use the computer, and so forth).

Speak slowly, as your tone of voice sends a message. Barking orders will produce a different result than speaking with an expectation. Children listen for hesitation or frustration, so do not be nervous or expect a tantrum because you will get one! Gently touch your child as you speak, which will provide a (nonverbal) message of importance.

## Recognition of Positives

Recognizing compliant, positive behaviors is the critical component that is needed to increase them. Recognition with a touch, along with a verbal narrative of what you see, will increase behavior and compliance. For example, you could say, "I see that you took your dishes to the sink!" or "I am proud of you for starting your homework right away." Remember the things you pay attention to will increase. If you are always finding fault, criticizing, or correcting, your child will learn to get your attention through negative ways. Make a point to recognize all positive behaviors with verbal praise or even just a quiet touch so those exact behaviors become habitual.

## Appropriate Consequences

When determining consequences, be mindful of your child's age and developmental capabilities. Consequences should not be frightening, demeaning, threatening, or hurtful. Effective consequences relate clearly to the misbehavior. Effective consequences teach a lesson.

For a baby who pulls hair while being held, an effective consequence is to immediately put the baby down. He will soon learn cause and effect, understanding that, when he pulls hair, he is no longer held. For a toddler who hits, an effective consequence is to help him learn to apologize while touching the person's area of hurt. He may require your hand-over-hand help to touch and your words of, "Johnny is sorry for hitting."

For an older child, a natural consequence for unacceptable behavior might be the elimination of privileges or services from you. Explain that, when he is out of control, he will lose all privileges until he can apologize for the exact behavior and then be accountable in some way (clean up, fix things, or do something to make it right). This is called a blackout. Explain that you will not respond to him, speak to him, drive him anywhere, or do anything for him until he is calm and able to apologize appropriately. Do not give in, and do be very consistent. Your ability to follow through will determine your success. Do this with love and kindness in an attempt to teach, not out of anger with the purpose of punishment. If you talk, negotiate, or shout, you will send a message that your child is powerful enough to make you angry and spin you out of control. Many parents are successful with the natural consequence of a blackout because most children of all ages seek one thing: parental love and attention. With love and attention, they will self-regulate and take responsibility within a very short time.

When a child gets nothing out of a behavior, he will stop. Your child will learn to comply and behave well only when there is no value in misbehaving. Children without an audience or someone to negotiate with will quickly learn how to behave.

## Mommy, I'm Bored!

Children display misbehaviors for a variety of reasons. The acronym HALT (hungry, angry, lonely, tired) can affect all of us. For a child, lonely can equate to being bored, which can very often ignite negative, attention-seeking behaviors. When a child is bored, he may misbehave in an attempt to force his parent to pay attention to him. It's sad but true; for a child, receiving negative attention (being yelled at or punished) is better than being ignored. Providing a child with age-appropriate exposure to new and positive experiences decreases his need for negative attention while improving his potential for self-regulating skills and higher academic learning in a school setting. Reading every day, touring your house together to identify different objects, teaching how to complete a small household task, or even going for a nature walk around the block will increase your young child's potential for learning, seeking, asking, and succeeding.

I work closely with parents who are concerned with their child's inappropriate or aggressive behaviors. Very often when I enter their homes, the TV is blaring with inappropriate music videos or an adult talk show with violent episodes. A young child who watches or overhears inappropriate programming cannot separate the information as right from wrong. He will receive it and, in one form or another, incorporate into his life. Some parents find the TV to be a great babysitter and keep cartoons and videos running all day, but children need more. Children are born to learn by doing, touching, and asking. Older children with more advanced cognitive and communication skills will actually tell their parent that they are bored, which is the opportune time to teach and provide new learning experiences. Typical responses of "Go outside and play!" or "You can always clean up your room!" do not provide a child with what he may be looking for, which is structure and some time with you.

Although it is often easier and faster to do things yourself, having small jobs, chores, and activities at the ready will ensure that your child doesn't become bored. Those activities will help him to feel important and build self-esteem, in addition to teaching a new skill. Include your child in your daily activities so he can learn how to do them independently with the very best of teachers: you!

## Build the Box

Assemble items with your child to create a decorated activity box. Place items in the box that your child can use independently: sidewalk chalk, bubbles, a new coloring book, or paint-by-water books with brushes. Use a brown paper bag for a nature hunt, with directions or a map to find ten special items right in your own backyard. An old piece of a cardboard box can become a wall mural for drawing family members. Place new items in the box often to maintain enthusiasm and excitement. Place several items in the activity box that require your attention, such as a simple craft, a box of Jell-O, or a bag of dry cookie dough mix that the two of you can prepare together. The next time your child says he is bored, remember that this is your opportunity to increase your child's independence, creativity, and life experiences. He's your child. Laugh, play, and teach!

# Gifts That Last a Lifetime

Buying toys and gifts for children has become a national pastime. So many parents buy a small prize each time they go to the store or purchase a new toy as a bribe. The true gifts, the ones that will shape a child, help him or her to grow, and last a lifetime, were written by Helene Rothschild, MA, MS, LMFT, and printed in her book *All You Need Is HART!*

Helene told me that a father once wrote to her, saying he purchased her poster with the words below and taped it to his son's bedroom door. The father said that every time he became angry with his son, he carefully read her words, which reminded him to teach his son rather than spank him.

Help Me Grow, Please …

Be consistent with me. Then I can trust your words and actions.
Comfort me when I'm scared, hurt, or sad. That will help me
feel I'm okay even when I'm not feeling strong or happy.
Take responsibility for all your feelings and actions. That will teach
me not to blame others and to take responsibility for my life.
Communicate what you feel hurt or frightened about when
you're angry at me. That helps me feel I'm a good person
and learn how to constructively deal with my feelings.
Tell me clearly and specifically what you want. Then it
is easier for me to hear you, and I will also know how
to communicate my needs in a positive way.
Express to me that I'm okay even when my words or behavior may not
be. That will help me learn from my mistakes and have high self-esteem.
Understand and accept me. I may be different than you, and I'm okay.
Balance your life between work and play. Then it is easier for me
to believe that I can grow up, be responsible, and still have fun.
Remember what you wanted when you were my age. Then
you'll better understand my needs and interests.
Treat me as an individual. That helps me believe that I can be my unique self.
Hug me and tell me that you care about me. That feels so good
and helps me to feel lovable and express caring to others.
Thank you for hearing me. I love you![3]

---

3  Helene Rothschild, *All You Need Is HART!* (Brandon, OR: Robert D. Reed Publishers, 2006), 100.

Our children watch us closely. They listen to our words, even if our words aren't meant for them. They do as we do, even if they shouldn't, perhaps because we have sent the wrong message or modeled a behavior without thinking about the effects it might have. Many things that our children do are done from their misunderstanding, not out of a conscious desire to misbehave. No child is a bad child. Teach your child with all your heart.

## True Stories

A group of preschoolers sat on the floor with musical instruments, which were piled in the center of the circle. The music teacher directed the children to run into the circle and choose their favorite instrument for the day. A very large child got up and ran for the tambourine, bumping into other little ones on his way to the center. The teacher admonished him in front of all the others. "What is wrong with you? Can't you see you've knocked over your classmates? You need to be more careful!" Although he did exactly what he was told, that experience brought unnecessary humiliation, making him uncomfortable and unmotivated to participate or even return to music class.

An eight-year-old sat in class with her peers, and when the teacher asked if there were any questions, she raised her hand and asked a question. The teacher said that was the most ridiculous question she had ever heard. She never answered the question, and that child never raised her hand in class again.

## Real Opportunities

Parents have the opportunity to give their child everything. I am not speaking of endless toys or throwaway collectibles. I am suggesting that parents give gifts that last a lifetime, gifts of who they are. Parents have the opportunity to fill their child with what their dreams were and what their dreams hold for them. They have the opportunity to show them, invite them, expose them, nurture them, and teach them. We are their teachers for life. They will do as we do. We are their heroes. We are their protectors. We are their heritage.

Parents have the opportunity to shape and mold their children, to instill in them the desire to dream and perhaps achieve all the things we did not. Sitting in front of the television will not help a child reach that dream. Every single day, a parent can start over and give his children the world. A parent has the opportunity to introduce and expose a child to anything and everything. It is important to take the job of a parent or educator seriously, providing each child with everything possible so he grows up to be all we had hoped for and more.

*A Tribute to Fathers*

My father was a New York City television director for *The Ed Sullivan Show* and *Sesame Street*. He traveled the world to direct Miss Universe and Miss America pageants, as well as NASA space launches and landings. He was a magnificent artist who exhibited in elite galleries, was featured in magazines, and sold to well-known actors and recording artists. He was strong and taught me jujitsu from his marine days. Charismatic and comfortable with celebrities, he was genuine. He taught me to follow my heart. He explained to me the pain and disappointment that we all endure throughout our lives makes small cracks in our hearts, which we need in order to make room for the joy and deep love to come. He never raised his hand or his voice. When I came in late, he asked why I missed curfew. My excuse was that I didn't have a watch so I lost track of time. He calmly replied that I would be allowed to go out with my friends when I earned enough money from babysitting to buy myself a watch. That was his way of grounding me, a lesson of natural consequences. He died twelve years ago, but he is with me every day.

I honor all fathers who have given their time or lives to fight for our safety. Working twelve miles outside of New York City on September 11 and watching the smoke for weeks after, I forever understand danger and fear and truly respect those who continue to protect us as they face it every day. Fathers are strong and protective, and they teach us about life. Some fathers want their children to experience life to the fullest, while others try to protect their child from every hurt. They are powerful role models. These two stories share a variety of perspectives.

# A Father's View

"When I think of fatherhood, I think about the children who must learn about hardship, isolation, fear, and even responsibility, experiences that affect them into adulthood," said our friend Rich Dever. "When Katie was born, I knew I wanted her to grow up never knowing fear, surrounded by people who love her and make her feel safe. For now, I have the responsibility and privilege of defining her world so she can become confident, independent, inquisitive, and kind. As she grows older, my responsibilities will change, and I will have to let her figure things out by herself. As she grows, I will help her understand the harshness that life sometimes has to offer. For now, goldfish live forever, and she is only 'scaredy' when it is followed by a giggle."

Great-grandfather Carl Pandoli said that, as a young father, providing for his family was most important to him. Although he sometimes worked late, he always kissed his children goodnight, even if they were fast asleep. His spoke of responsibility and protection. I watch him now as he continues to guide his adult children and grown grandchildren. He is a soft touch as he offers wisdom. Now, as a great-grandfather, he gently holds Sophia with pure love and joy, who once fit in the palm of his large hand.

My husband, Robert, describes his father as a proud man who built his success with hard work, ensuring that his children lived a better life than he had. A proud sergeant in the airborne division of the army, he returned from war to teach his children the importance of family and honor. He saved for their college, working late nights as a drummer in a big band to supplement his day job as an upholsterer. Although some could see only his military side, he displayed a fun, loving side by splurging on ice cream cones and coddling his grandchildren. He carried his unending love for his wife, Mary, Robert's mom, until the day he died.

I asked Robert's grown children to share their thoughts of their dad. Over the years, Robert has become a role model for his children. They described him as a gentle guardian and willing teacher:

> He created excitement and wonders by building a tree house onto our shed and provided endless fun by throwing us around in the town lake. He was the teacher who quizzed us during summer break, keeping our brains active. He was the comedian who wore his Goofy hat all over Disney World, even though he looked silly. As we have grown older, Dad has become someone to share precious moments and enjoyable meals with. He is the one who gives sound advice. He gives it without judgment, with a lot of thought and love. He is an unshakable pillar of strength and knowledge. He gives his love unconditionally and leads by his words and his actions. I hope that, as I move further into adulthood, I will carry some of my dad's strength, kindness, and generosity. When others

say I remind them of my dad, I smile and beam with pride. A father is someone who has children, but a dad is a parent with compassion and a role model. Father's Day is one day a year to say thanks, but I am grateful for my dad three hundred sixty-five days a year.

To all dads, we thank you for all you have given to us.

## A Tribute to Mothers

Even in difficult economic times, there still is a job worth taking with lasting rewards. It is being a mom.

**Job Description:** Family management specialist who is completely dedicated, energetic, enthusiastic, creative, and patient; able to multitask, inspire, redirect, listen, teach, assess crises, negotiate, meet multiple needs at one time, and build self-esteem through consistent, positive reinforcement, selfless love, and tenderness with the innate ability to nurture. Experience in entry-level first aid is preferred. Financial management of household expenses is beneficial.

**Requirements:** No experience necessary

**Hours:** Full time, twenty-four hours per day, seven days per week

**Vacation/Personal Days:** None

**Salary:** $0

**Benefits:** Unlimited and endless

The history of Mother's Day began with a group of mothers, dating around 1870, joining together for their common cause, to support one another for those whose sons had fought and/or died in the Civil War. The first official Mother's Day was celebrated in Philadelphia on May 10, 1908. It is not simply another opportunity for card companies to make money, but instead a day to celebrate and honor all mothers, maternal bonds, and motherhood itself.

Sharon Nittinger, life coach and presenter with Nittinger Seminars in Stow, Ohio, urges moms to give themselves permission to consider their own needs. Sharon said, "Remembering the person you are outside of motherhood is empowering. By connecting with your inner self, you are better equipped at managing the stressors of motherhood, and you strengthen your mothering abilities. When I give presentations on motherhood, moms repeatedly comment about feeling guilty when taking time for themselves. I remind them that they have a very difficult job and everyone deserves time away from work. Even the president takes vacations."

I identify with the mothers who pace the floors night after night and those who pray endlessly for their child's health and future. I respectfully honor the mothers who solemnly pray for peace and those who endure unimaginable pain. There are moms who cry endlessly out of love for their child and those who laugh with enough joy to fill a room. I believe that, once a mother, always a mother, no matter whose mother you are. Mothers are powerful, soft, and gentle. Mothers shape us into who we become. Mothers make us cry, teach us how to love, and give us strength.

I am the lucky mother of three wonderful adult children. My deep love for my children, an incomprehensible, indescribable, unconditional love, has led me through feelings of overwhelming responsibility, emotional highs and lows, heartaches, self-doubt, and sleepless nights. The love for my children is never-ending, as our bond grows stronger with each day. My most prized accomplishment is having raised them to become who they are: thoughtful, self-confident, successful adults.

I am fortunate to have a wonderful mother who is the epitome of grace and dignity. She modeled strong moral values and selfless love as she taught my sister and me how to navigate the roads of life. Her endless love and emotional support inspired me to pursue each and every one of my dreams. Nearly three years ago, when I relocated from the East Coast to the Midwest, I asked my mom to give up all she knew and join me in the adventure of starting another life chapter in a new location. She did! My mother is also my dear friend. I honor and treasure her love and her friendship.

Happy Mother's Day to every woman who has been lucky enough to be called "Mom."

## Dear Diana

*Building a Relationship*

_Dear _Diana, I read your articles regularly and love the patient approach that you bring to raising children. I grew up in the era of spanking and yelling, so changing those ways is sometimes difficult. Advice like yours helps in changing these behaviors. I am writing because I need some advice on changing how I interact with our eleven-year-old son. I get so frustrated with his behavior that I often find myself treating him in ways that I would never treat anyone else nor want to be treated myself. We do a lot of yelling at each other, and I am concerned that it is having dramatic consequences. In fact, when I read stories about how kids his age are committing suicide, I think that could very easily be our son. He has always struggled over the years with bullying by other kids, and unfortunately, the school has done little to help with the problem. We are considering changing schools in hopes that it will improve, but we want to correct his habits and mine when it comes to our reaction to each other. Please help.

.Dear Mom, It is difficult to change how we view things as well as how we do things, so you deserve great credit as you strive to change. Awareness, intention, and motivation are the foundation for change, and it seems you have all three. You have an awareness of your actions, how you would like to change your actions toward your son, the impact of your actions, as well as the impact of the actions of others through bullying. Your intention is to have a good relationship without yelling or harsh treatment. To change that, you need to stop yelling, learn to communicate calmly, set boundaries, hear his concerns, and increase your bond, that is, connect with love. That is a lot of change. However, step by step, you can make those changes. Your motivation is to have a relationship with your son. Parents sometimes lose sight of their love for their child because they are caught up in the problems their child is causing, seeing him only as the root of their stress. Children read their parent's gestures, movements, and facial features like an open book. Those expressions formulate a perception for a child. He may perceive that he is the problem, which becomes a reality when he misbehaves. Tweens and teens are emotionally fragile, and yes, tragically, some do commit suicide when they feel they do not feel heard or understood. Be there for your son, no matter what.

*Making Positive Changes*

- **Stop yelling.** Just stop. When you are angry or hear yourself yelling, take in a big breath and close your mouth. Then exhale slowly. Take a moment to compose yourself. Pat yourself on the back for stopping an unproductive and destructive behavior.

- **Learn to communicate.** Speak in a factual tone of voice, lower your volume, and speak calmly, as a loving parent who teaches. Use the phrase, "I'm sorry you feel that way, but my answer is the same." Or say, "I am very angry right now. I will give you my answer after lunch." Express your concerns and your feelings often. Teach him to express his feelings appropriately in conversation. Talk as much as you can.

- **Set boundaries by teaching, modeling, and following through.** Calmly communicate consequences that fit the action. Explain that you will not be yelling nor will you participate in any yelling communication. When he forgets and yells, quietly remind him that he may talk to you when he is able to speak quietly. Then walk away.

- **Listen and learn.** Do not make assumptions or try to fix everything. Ask him how he feels, and ask for details. When he is angry or frustrated, ask him what he can do for a different result. Problem solve together. Really listen so he feels heard and valued. When you talk, stand or sit near him so he can feel your support. Reach out to physically connect as you communicate.

- **Build a relationship.** As you begin to communicate in a positive way, you will see that he will begin to open up and let you in. The more you do together and the more you talk with each other, the easier it will be to do just that.

# 2

# Child Development

## Introduction: From Birth through Five Years Old

This chapter is presented through a series of articles, each of which provide a generalized overview of the needs, expectations, and development of a child from birth through five years old. As each child develops at his own pace, your child may reach a particular milestone slightly before or after another child within the same age range. Always contact your pediatric office with questions or concerns.

These young years provide the foundation of who your child will grow up to be, as his personality and interests evolve and self-esteem begins to build. Ninety percent of brain growth occurs within the first three years of life.[4] Your child is listening, watching, processing, and gathering information at all times. Impressions, experiences, and exposure are all collected into his brain bank for processing. What you say and how you say it matter a great deal as you shape your child's world. You are providing the scaffolding for his future years.

The things you do, as well as how you respond to your child, will determine much of his behavior. Some parents may become frustrated with their one-year-old who cries often or has difficulty sleeping. Others may become disappointed or embarrassed with their two-year-old who never shares or their three-year-old who has meltdowns in public. This chapter offers a general understanding of what your child is and is not capable of comprehending. You will understand that two-year-olds are developmentally incapable of sharing, as they are learning how to navigate

---

4   *I Am Your Child: The First Years Last Forever*

through their world and protect what they take ownership of. Having that knowledge and knowing that your child is not intentionally being selfish can help you to respond differently and redirect him with a positive outcome.

Children behave as they do because of several factors, including age, their need for attention, their developmental capabilities, past experiences, or perhaps a medical compromise. It is important to understand that children generally do not intend to be selfish, mean, or demanding. They do not set out to be hurtful or bad. They have learned how to behave through prior interactions provided by their role models: parents, caregivers, extended family, older siblings, and so forth. Understanding your child's developmental capabilities will help to find teaching opportunities. These are opportunities where you can provide simple communication or redirection that your child is able to understand, process, and respond to. Although maturity cannot be forced, consistent, thoughtful exposure to age-appropriate information with developmentally appropriate expectations will help him obtain and maintain the social and emotional skills he needs for healthy development.

Babies are a most precious gift given to our care. The relationship you build with your child during his young years will determine how you connect with him in his teen years and later into adulthood. Close family ties are built during the early years of development, so spend the extra time and patiently make time for those moments when you are able to provide your child with everything he needs.

## Wired at Birth

Congratulations! Becoming a parent is a precious gift. You provide your child's comfort and warmth. You are his teacher for life. Your child is wired to develop social skills, trust, and healthy relationships. He is ready to develop communication skills to express and receive information correctly and appropriately. His overall emotional temperament is ready to absorb information. You need to be vigilant with your physical and emotional protection of your child, always cognizant of exactly what you are exposing him to.

## *Brain Development*

When my first child was nearing his first birthday, I read about rapid brain development as it occurs within the first three years of life. I felt I had lost one of his precious three years, as it was almost over. As a teacher by training, from his birth, I had focused on providing him with nurturing, yet age-appropriate, stimulating experiences. Without even realizing how precious and impressionable his first year of brain development had been, I provided consistent exposure to appropriate experiences, with the underpinnings of a predictable, loving environment. It is never too late to focus on your child's social, emotional, or functional development.

Some parents wonder if they are spoiling their baby by picking him up too often, picking him up whenever he cries, or holding him for too long. Babies have critical needs that must be met in order to help them learn to self-regulate and bond. Babies need to be held, rocked, soothed, fed, and changed in a timely manner in order to learn to trust and attachment. Parents who whisper, read, talk, and sing to their babies communicate and teach his new spoken language, as babies are wired and ready at birth to learn any language.

## *Your New Baby*

Your beautiful new baby is an individual, so to compare his development with another baby his age can produce unnecessary and unhealthy stress.[5] Two children raised within the same home may have completely different personalities, sleep patterns, food likes or dislikes, motor or athletic abilities, intellectual capabilities, and so forth. One baby may crawl at an earlier age before another, who may be focusing on language and communication skills. These are not things with which to be overly concerned as long as they are within the normal range of development. Contact your pediatrician with any concerns, as guidelines are available for typical development. Although some children may develop different skills earlier than or a bit later than what a guideline may suggest, those children will still fall within the threshold of the normal range.

---

5 *Touchpoints: The Essential Reference*, 51.

## Basic Needs

Over the next six months, as your newborn moves into infancy and then into babyhood, you will see remarkable surges of development in all areas. Take lots of pictures because you will want to hold on to these precious moments forever.

## Cognitive Development

Your baby needs to sleep, to be properly fed, and to have his basic needs met for healthy development. Diluting formula or reusing the remains of an old bottle to save money can cause long-term functional damage. You hold a very precious life in your arms, so it is important to reach out for help if you are overwhelmed or overtired. The strong, courageous parent seeks information or help when she feels she can't provide everything her baby needs.

Babies are wired at birth to learn any language, and yours will be listening intently. Provide repeated soft sounds, quiet talking, and soft music. Read books for your baby to hear the intonation of his language. He will stare at faces, locking in and seeking information from your eyes. Within the first two months, he will begin to recognize familiar faces.

A study was done where a mom sang "Twinkle Twinkle Little Star" with excited eyes and facial expressions. Her baby watched intently and gurgled with excitement. When she sang it again without any facial expression and no eye movement, her baby became unsettled, turned his head away, looked back to see if her expressions had changed, and then began to cry when he couldn't read her expressions. Babies learn to read facial expressions and attempt to self-regulate very early on.[6]

## Other Senses

Within the first few days, a newborn will be able to recognize the scent of his mother or primary caregiver as she approaches. As a newborn, he is sensitive to bright light, which may cause him to sneeze when he first opens his eyes, as the nerves in his sinuses and eyes adjust to the visual stimulation. By about two months old, your infant should start to follow objects with his eyes and will develop a social smile. Your baby will be able to see objects from eight to fifteen inches in front of him, and he will focus

---

6   *I Am Your Child: The First Years Last Forever*

briefly on moving objects as far as three feet away. At this age, he prefers black and white or high contrast patterns as opposed to pastels. He will bring objects to his mouth for exploration, and by the four- to six-month mark, as he chews on things, he will also shake and bang those objects to figure out what they do.[7]

Nearing three months old, your baby will be kicking with strength and placing his fist in his mouth. He will be able to hold an object for a short time as he watches his own hand movements and waves his arms wildly. As arm strength increases, by about five months, he may push up with his arms from a tummy position. Approaching six months, your baby may be sitting (with or without hand support), rolling both ways (from front to back and back to front), transferring objects from one hand to the other, and reaching with one hand for objects. By the age of six months, your baby will have developed full color vision and have the ability to track moving objects.

## Language Development

Dr. T. Berry Brazelton did a study with a newborn, only five days old, to determine the baby's ability to connect and communicate. He held the newborn between himself and its mom in a competition for the baby's attention. They both spoke at the same time to the baby in a quiet voice, repeating the same words over and over, "What a beautiful little baby you are." The baby turned his head toward his mom immediately, as he recognized and was comforted by her voice, which he had come to know during the past nine months before his birth. When the study was done immediately after, with the doctor and the dad competing, the newborn chose his father, whose voice he had also become familiar with while in utero.[8]

Dr. Brazelton also found that from early on, when you pay close attention, you will be able to distinguish between your baby's cries of hunger, overstimulation, discomfort, or need for sleep.[9] Watch your baby when he yawns. Is he tired, or is he overstimulated and trying to detach? Crying is your baby's language, so listen closely as he tries to communicate with you. By three months old, your baby's crying will diminish and be replaced with pleasurable sounds, including laughing, giggling, and

---

7  *Touchpoints: The Essential Reference*, 79.
8  *Touchpoints: The Essential Reference*, 34.
9  Ibid., 42, 72.

continuous cooing.[10] By four months, he will respond to you with gurgling and cooing. Communicate through touch as your baby processes soft, gentle stroking as a form of love and caring. By five months, he may blow raspberries and attempt to repeat sounds, and by six months, he will make identifying sounds to express his discomfort or pleasure. By the end of six months, your baby will begin to respond to the word "no" and will be able to distinguish your emotions by your tone of voice.

## *Putting Sounds Together*

Your baby will begin to babble chains of consonants. It is interesting to note that all sounds made by all infants are similar, regardless of the language spoken in the home. These are critical months for you to expose your baby to language, through quiet talking, songs, and stories with pictures to identify objects. Introduce your version of animal noises matched with pictures as a form of a simple baby sign language. Soon, he will scrunch up his nose and sniff with delight when you ask, "What does the bunny say?" Blowing raspberries, squealing, and growling are identified as expansion babbling, which occur between four and six months.[11]

## Six to Twelve Months

So much growth and development occurs between six months to a year. Treasure these months as your baby learns to move around and explore his world. Watch closely as his personality emerges through these next few months.

## *Cognitive Development*

By six months, your baby will begin to learn that he can attract attention by expressing his needs, wants, and interests. He will have learned that when he cries, someone will come. He will explore with both his eyes and his hands. He will begin to show genuine affection toward his primary caregiver. You may notice that stranger anxiety is evident around eight months, but that will pass.

Your baby will start to develop the concept of object permanence. That means he can locate a partially hidden object that you have hidden while

---

10   Ibid., 47, 60.
11   *Infancy: Infant, Family, and Society*, 252.

he was watching.[12] He will start to use simple gestures, such as shaking his head to communicate "no." At this young age, your baby will begin to look for the correct picture in a book when it is named. He will start to respond to his own name and become interested with what happens when he repeatedly drops or bangs items.

By ten months, your baby may visibly begin to express his moods, expressing whether he is happy, sad, fearful, or excited. By twelve months, he will want to explore your cupboards, dump and pick up objects, look for and find hidden toys, point to things he wants, learn to blow kisses, and "come to mommy." This is such an exciting time as he becomes more capable of communicating his wants and needs.

## Physical Development

Physical development is a big area of growth during these six months. Your baby will grasp, hold, and release objects as he develops an understanding of cause and effect. By around eight months, he will start to self-feed with purpose and begin to crawl. Physically, he may be sitting up without support, pivoting around on his stomach, transferring toys from one hand to the other, creeping or pulling himself along the floor, poking fingers into tiny holes, putting on and taking off lids, as well as placing and removing objects from containers. He may possibly climb to a height of six inches and cruise along the furniture to gain balance for those first few steps.[13] This is an extremely critical time for safety-proofing.[14] Get on your hands and knees and crawl around to see what your baby is seeing. You may find dangers seen from floor level that were not evident from a standing or sitting position. Safety-proof every electrical outlet, remove unstable furniture, and relocate sharp or dangerous items to unreachable heights in order to protect your child. His sudden mobility, which could put him in danger, will amaze you. Your child's life is in your hands, so never leave him unattended.

## Language Development

Your baby will deliberately vocalize, both for practice as well as to view your reaction. He will babble in long strings of syllables (dadada, mamama,

---

12   *Touchpoints: The Essential Reference*, 127.
13   *Infancy: Infant, Family, and Society*, 274.
14   *Touchpoints: The Essential Reference*, 109.

gagaga), using inflections and exclamations, including "uh-oh!"[15] His cry will have a different, distinguishable pitch for various needs such as hunger, hurt, or fatigue, so listen closely as he tries to communicate with you. By around nine months, you may note that your baby will echo sounds and may show an increased receptive understanding of words such as "no-no." Nearing eleven months, you may hear your baby experiment with his first words. I introduced sign language to my son when he was about six months old. By about eleven months old, he was able to communicate that he wanted to take a bath or have a drink through sound and gesture. I taught him what a horse does, capitalizing on his ability to blow raspberries. When asked what a butterfly does, he batted and blinked his eyes. For a bunny, he sniffed and scrunched his nose. I taught him traditional sign language for words, including water, milk, and more. It is truly remarkable to see a young child communicate through gesture. Take time to read to your baby every day, exposing him to new words and new pictures. Walk through your house and talk about what you are seeing and hearing. Go outside to ring the doorbell. Then let him push it and say, "Ding-dong! Doorbell!" The more you talk to your child, the more information he will obtain and process.

## Happy First Birthday!

Your baby has grown into toddlerhood! Remarkable development in communication, fine and large motor abilities, and more complex cognitive thinking skills will fill this next year. Stay focused on your toddler's safety as well as the many stimulating experiences you can provide for him.

*Cognitive Development*

Your toddler will become increasingly more aware of himself and slowly become interested in the company of others. This is an excellent time to introduce a playgroup, a small circle of friends within the same age range who can explore and learn together. Toddlers of this age will play alongside each other, known as parallel play. They will compete for toys and enjoy watching each other. Children are unable to share until well into their threes, so provide plenty of interesting items for everyone to explore. Be prepared to redirect your little one when someone has the toy he wants. Your toddler will imitate the behaviors of others, so be mindful of what you say and do. Most likely, many things that your child sees and

---

15 *Infancy: Infant, Family, and Society*, 252.

hears will be repeated when you least expect it. This is also the beginning of limit testing, so be consistent and follow through. When you take something away from your toddler or remove him from a dangerous situation, he may object by crying. He may even return to the restricted area and ignore your warnings. Teach with consistency, and choose your battles carefully. Reserve the word "no" for the most important dangerous occasions. Remove items, remove your child, and distract him with an interesting item or a silly song, but be vigilant with his safety.

Approaching eighteen months, your toddler may choose "no" as his favorite word. He may protest loudly and challenge you with a tantrum. Do not take it personally. Remain in calm, teaching frame of mind. Understand that how you handle each meltdown will determine the length, level, and frequency in which they occur. You will also begin to see your toddler's sense of independence and self-confidence strengthen, while some episodes of separation anxiety may increase by his second birthday. Within these later months, toward the age of two, your toddler will be showing signs of possessiveness, often using the word "mine." He may cry when a toy is removed or object loudly when he sees that your attention is drawn toward another child. This is very typical, healthy development. Your toddler simply needs reassurance regarding the things important to him, including your love.

## Physical Development

You may notice that your child's physical growth rate has become less rapid. However, his fine and gross motor skill development will astound you. He will be able to walk unassisted while pulling a toy behind him. He will also gain steady balance as he pushes a larger item, such as a toy lawn mower or doll stroller.[16] He will carry a large toy while walking, kick a ball, stand on tiptoes, climb up on high places, and use stairs while supported. His fine motor skills will include scribbling and turning objects such as knobs and pages. He will open and turn over a container to pour its content and build a tower of four or more blocks. Watch for signs of right- or left-hand dominance during this time. With all this mobility, it is critical that your toddler never be left alone. A second round of childproofing should be done on your hands and knees to see the world as he does.

---

16 *Developmental Profiles: Pre-Birth Through Eight*, 73–74.

*Language Development*

Between the ages of one and two years, your toddler will be able to understand much of what you say. Be very mindful that he is listening and processing, just waiting to use those words. By providing a good language model, your toddler will master at least fifty spoken words.[17] Initially, the beginning consonant of each word should be understandable, while immediate family may only recognize the full pronunciation. Provide lots of praise repeating each word correctly as your toddler begins to speak. You may begin to notice that your toddler's receptive language, what he is able to understand, accelerates as he responds to your simple statements of the following: naptime, time to eat, or "Where is the puppy?" By his second birthday, he should be able to respond to names of familiar people, locate items you refer to, follow simple directives, repeat words, and speak in two- to four-word sentences.

# The Terrific Twos!

It's a whirlwind year ahead with a two-year-old who loves a certain food one day and decides he will have none of it the next day! Coaxing or begging your child will simply teach him that he holds some power in keeping your attention. Your approach to managing meltdowns will teach your toddler how to behave. Although this year is often referred to as "terrible twos," I refer to it as the "terrific twos" because so much learning is going on. Endless potential, ever-increasing motor skills, social development, and a brilliant little mind that continues to develop at a rapid rate will fill your toddler.

*Cognitive Development*

Two-year-olds learn quickly through imitation. They watch others cut the lawn and practice their skills with a child-sized plastic lawn mower to push. They watch as the vacuum moves back and forth across the rug and work side by side with their toy vacuum or hand vac. They talk with perfect intonation using a toy phone and learn to steer a toy car. They imitate behavior and language, acting out what they see and repeating what they hear. Make-believe play is an integral part of learning at this age, so provide plenty of opportunity for

---

17  *Developmental Profiles: Pre-Birth Through Eight*, 75.

pretending.[18] Listen to your child as he talks to his teddy bear or doll. Chances are that you will hear him repeat the same words he has heard from you.

This is a magical time, as your child is now starting to learn about his feelings, which become integrated with the limits and boundaries you set. Toddlers of this age rely on consistent routine, learning from repetition and understanding what is expected of them. A two-year-old learns to navigate through the world around him as he learns how to get his own needs met. Developmentally, a two-year-old is unable to share, and without much control over his emotions, he can become easily upset when he doesn't get what he wants. When he does want something, he will watch closely for your response. Your response will teach him how to respond. He may cry relentlessly, learning whether you will follow through or how long he needs to cry before he will get what he wants. Some parents bend, change the rules, or give in to tantrums because it is easier at that time. However, providing the same answers or responses each time will teach your toddler that there is no reason to push because you won't bend.

Your child will begin to understand initial concepts of time (now, later, before, and after) and placement (in, out, up, down, over, and under). He will learn to match similar objects and classify them into groupings. By the time he turns three, he will be able to build with six to ten blocks, complete a four-piece puzzle, and sort by color and shape. Toileting, sleep patterns, and promoting positive behaviors are typical challenges that parents face during this year. Focus on building confidence by recognizing successes so he becomes secure enough to develop some independence.

## Physical Development

Within this year, you can expect your child to be able to walk and run with ease. He will climb and descend stairs using alternate footing and be able to kick a ball. He will master a tricycle and propel himself with his feet in a desired direction on a riding toy. His eye-hand coordination will increase as he uses a crayon to draw circular motions and horizontal and vertical lines. He will not be able to stay within the lines of a coloring book, so freestyle drawing or imagination painting may be more appealing. His fine motor skills will become more exact over time, but for now, you can watch him concentrate as he refines his finger movements. Using new large motor abilities, running away from your side may become a game, so protect your child by teaching him to hold your hand. Play running games often, and

---

18  *Developmental Profiles: Pre-Birth through Eight*, 84.

provide lots of praise when he follows your directions. Teach him to learn when to run and when to stop. The Building Skills chapter has tools to teach your child to remain with you and safely hold your hand.

## Language Development

Exciting times are ahead as you and your child become better able to communicate. He will comprehend much of what you tell him, provided you speak in simple phrases with simple directives. Use only three to four words in a sentence, and provide all your information in three sentences or less, emphasizing adjectives and verbs. "Why" questions emerge at this age. Whether this becomes frustrating or funny, answer your child with a simple one-line answer.[19] If you need to provide more information than can be offered in three sentences, stop. Allow time for your child to process what you said before offering more information. He will learn to follow two- and three-step directions and will soon speak in four- to five-word sentences, using the following words in the correct context: I, you, me, and they. Decide now how you want your child to refer to himself. Many parents use their child's name in conversation, such as, "Is Nathan hungry?" rather than "Are you hungry?" Your child will learn to speak as you have taught him.

By three years old, your child will use up to six words in a sentence. Within his sentences, he will name common objects, familiar faces, places he enjoys, and foods he wants. He will make his needs known in recognizable language by forming words correctly. Speak to him throughout the day about what you are doing. Read to him continuously with intonation, identifying objects, and using proper pronunciation. This will promote increased language development. Your toddler will be able to follow a story line and remember many ideas and characters in a book, so read, read, read. He will also begin to have fun with jokes, rhymes, and silly songs, so help him develop his sense of humor as you sing, read, and giggle together.

## "Mine!"

We recently had our friends for a Sunday afternoon dinner with their absolutely delightful two-year-old daughter. We've been watching Miss Katie grow from babyhood, and we thoroughly enjoy everything about her. She talks a mile a minute, completely unfiltered and innocently uninhibited.

---

19 *Infancy: Infant, Family, and Society*, 395.

Katie seems far more intelligent than her two little years, questioning and referencing things that simply amaze me. When I admired her shoes, she explained in detail where she got them. She counted to ten in both English and Spanish. She ate with manners, followed her mom's directive of "food stays in the kitchen," explored our home carefully, and entertained us with songs. Katie was also able to keep herself busy, reading books and quietly feeding her baby doll hors d'oeuvres, saying, "Try this, baby. You will like it!" She moved easily from her dad's lap to her mom's and then back to her dad's. I melted when she climbed into my lap. She giggled excitedly as my husband played tricks to entertain her, pulling M&M's from behind her ear. She galloped around in a cowboy hat, squealing, "Yee-ha!"

I'd forgotten how delightful life is through the eyes of a two-year-old. Then it happened. It got close to bedtime. The meltdowns started with a few defiant "nos." Her parents corrected her, reminding her of her manners, but then along with "No!" came the words, "It's mine!" There isn't much one can do when a toddler becomes overtired. As we quickly finished our dinner, she endured our conversation while eating her ice cream. After finishing her ice cream, she clearly expressed her desire for chocolate, saying "Mine! That's mine!" With a little distraction, we quieted and comforted her on a soft couch with her baby doll as her parents packed up the car to leave. Before they left, I asked our friends if they had ever heard of Murphy's Law for Toddlers. For those of you with a two-year-old, and for those who have raised one, this is for you.

## Murphy's Law for Toddlers

If it is mine, it is mine.

If it is yours, it is mine.

If I like it, it is mine.

If I can take it from you, it is mine.

If I am playing with it, all of the pieces are mine.

If I think it is mine, it is.

If I saw it first, it is mine.

If I had it first, it is mine.

If I had it and put it down, it is still mine.

If you had it and put it down, it is now mine.

If it looks like the one I have at home, it is mine.

If it is broken, it is yours.[20]

Enjoy every minute. It does go by so quickly!

---

20  www.murphys-laws.com/murphy/murphy-toddler.htm

# Preschoolers

Welcome to the world of preschoolers. This is an amazing time where your child will learn to identify numbers and letters, write his name, understand cause and effect, display increased social skills, verbalize his feelings, and show the world his ever-emerging personality. So many parents express frustration with a child of this age due to seemingly endless temper tantrums, a lack of sleep, and the necessary time-consuming hours that a preschooler requires. Trust me, this is nothing compared to the experience of raising an adolescent. Learn to embrace tantrums, and turn them into valuable teaching opportunities. Stay focused and teach with love and limits so you will be able to enjoy all of your precious moments together.

## Cognitive Development

Your preschooler learns everything about the world around him through what he sees, hears, touches, tastes, smells, and feels. He remains a concrete learner so his perception, his understanding of things, may not be the reality of the situation. A concrete thinker will choose a large glass half-filled with water rather than a small glass filled to the top. He will also choose ten pennies over a dime because it is more. Abstract thinking develops in a few years, so be patient in your understanding and provide simple explanations. Adults and other children in his life are role models, so surround your child with those whose morals and values you respect and admire.

Identifying feelings for your preschooler will help him learn to communicate his needs and frustrations. When setting limits, you might say, "It's okay to be upset, but you may not be rude." Identify and confirm his feelings with sentences such as, "I understand you feel upset," or "You must feel so proud of yourself for the way you behaved." Always provide a nurturing, loving environment that will help him to develop self-confidence, leading to trust and security, while furthering his independence.

Fears or anxieties may develop between the ages of three and five. Your child's emotions or fears should never be diminished through the following thoughtless remarks:

- "Don't be such a baby."
- "Only babies cry."
- "Don't be ridiculous. There's nothing to be afraid of."

Validating your child's feelings is a critical component in helping him learn how to comfortably approach you in future years with his concerns, fears, and questions. This is the time to build your scaffolding for open communication, which will impact your overall relationship. You may be surprised when a new awareness in sexuality emerges. Address situations simply and clearly, answering your preschooler directly with one or two sentences to satisfy his curiosity. I have written about typical fears and how they can be managed in the Fears chapter.

Children between the ages of three and five years often display behavior that is troubling to parents, for example, biting, noncompliance, tantrums, or a tendency to whine or cry often. Choose one behavior you would like to better manage, determine an effective plan of action with positive incentives (not bribes), and follow through in a loving way with consistency. Be aware of potential underlying causes that might include sensory concerns, overstimulation, or being overly tired so you can provide the best environment for your child's success. Power struggles over eating, sleeping, and toileting may emerge. Your child has more control in these areas than you do, so be thoughtful with how you handle these situations. Forceful demands may only provoke a challenge and extend the problem. By five, your child will have more control over his emotions. He will look for limits and be capable of accepting them if they have been consistently provided. This is a great age to introduce simple, concrete house rules.

## Physical Development

Preschoolers set challenges for themselves and look for an audience to appreciate their achievements. They love to show off how high they can jump or how fast they can run. Large motor skills are solid and well balanced, enabling them to run, gallop, skip, stand on one foot, roller-skate, ride a bike, and pump on a swing.[21] Remain vigilant regarding your preschooler's safety. Increased mobility and independence can be a dangerous combination when a ball goes rolling into the street. You may think your child is capable of playing alone in the yard, but he hasn't developed the maturity to make safe decisions. By late four or early five, he will have developed a sharp fine motor grip with pencils and crayons, enabling him to stay within the lines and cut with scissors. Early exposure to these materials will help his level of mastery for cutting and writing skills. Provide a basket of art and craft materials that will spark his interest.

---

21  *Infancy: Infant, Family, and Society*, 380.

When washable markers, glue, crayons, and paints are at the ready, there is no limit to what your child can create with his imagination and his busy little hands.

## Language Development

By three, you will be well into the "why?" stage. Three-year-olds use nearly one thousand words and expressions. They speak with intonation and expression with all understanding 90 percent of their language. By four, a typical child uses about fifteen hundred words in context and speaks in four-word sentences. Your child may chatter or attempt to engage in conversations with older children and adults. He is continuing to build upon his vocabulary, listen for intonation, and increase his expressive language skills. You may hear expressions, including "what if" or "suppose I" as he models adult conversations. Continuously provide books, read to your child often, and offer simple one- or two-word picture books regularly so he can read with independence. By five, a typical child will have an expressive word bank of two thousand words and receptively understand more than ten thousand words. You can expect longer sentences with the following connectors: but, and, and because. This high-level language may lead a parent to think of his child as much older or more capable than he really is. Remember that your five-year-old is still learning, developing, and modeling whatever he sees or hears. This is also the age where shock value is tested, and your child may say or do disturbing things that he has seen or heard. Children will often use language specifically to obtain a reaction. How you handle disturbing words or actions will determine the extent to which he continues to use them.

Enjoy every minute, take a breath when you need to, follow through with love and consistency, and take pride in your many achievements as a parent.

# Dear Diana

## Teach Your Preschooler How to Apologize

Dear Diana, My almost three-year-old is starting to get really angry with me, sometimes spewing, "I hate you ... I don't like you ... No, I don't want you." Any suggestions on reactions I should be giving? I'm doing a lot of, "I love you, and I know you love me too." I tried ignoring her. I tried telling her that she may not use those words because those are not nice words. Yikes! Kind of early for this, isn't it? What happened to my sweet little girl? Disheartened Mom

⌒

Dear Disheartened Mom, It is truly heartbreaking when your own child says hurtful things. Know that you are not alone and most parents have heard hurtful words from their children at one time or another. It seems unbelievable that a child can so calmly say such ugly things with all we do for them. However, eliminating that behavior is possible once you understand it. To answer your question: No, it's not too early for her to be spewing. As long as she can talk, she can spew. Developmentally, she is right on track. She is entering an age of great independence. Three-year-olds become very social and learn by doing, watching, talking, and waiting for reactions. Your reaction is critical in teaching her how to behave. It helps to know where she is hearing these phrases. Even innocent G-rated movies include strong words and emotions. Identify the source to eliminate it, or reference it when you are correcting her. You mentioned that you tried ignoring her. Never ignore unacceptable behavior. Every unacceptable behavior must be addressed in order to teach a child that it is unacceptable. How you teach will directly affect your outcome. Do not take it personally, or you will be less effective as her teacher.

- **Step One.** When she says, "I don't like you!" go to her, bend down, hold her shoulders, and say, "You may not say, 'I don't like you.'" Then walk away. If you are out, do the same, but (obviously) don't leave her. Do not interact with her until she acknowledges her mistake. Initially, she may not process your response and may make a request such as asking for a cookie or going outside to play. Bend down and say, "I can help you after you apologize for saying 'I don't like you.'" Then walk away. She will eventually understand that she must apologize before getting what she wants. When she starts to cry because she isn't getting her cookie, offer verbal cues, once more saying, "I can help you when you say, 'I'm sorry for saying I don't like you.'" Do not say, "I know you didn't mean that." That opens the door for power struggles such as, "Yes, I do!" Do not say, "That's mean. I love you no matter what." That sends a confusing message. Sometimes, a parent will avoid confronting a child for fear of a power struggle or an escalated temper tantrum. However, you will not like what evolves over the next few years if it is not lovingly and carefully addressed now.

- **Step Two.** The moment she apologizes in any manner, accept her apology, and give her a hug, saying, "I accept your apology for saying 'I don't like you.'" Tell her it is okay to feel mad or sad, but she may not say hurtful words. Then drop it. Later in the day, your only reference should be praise and reinforcement for her nice apology.

- **Step Three.** There are stages of apologies. Apologizing is a skill that needs to be taught. It does not come naturally. Initially, accept any apology in any tone of voice as long as it includes the exact behavior. After a handful of these apologies, move to the next lesson, teaching her to apologize in a nice voice with a touch. Teach her to gently touch you and say, "I'm sorry I said I don't like you." Your response should always be to bend down, accept her apology, and give a gentle touch, hug, or kiss. You are teaching your daughter to apologize in small, incremental steps with two goals: learning to apologize and having self-regulation to eliminate unkind words. She needs to feel good about her apology. You can teach her to come back often to apologize, so accept with open arms whenever she does.

You sound like a great mom. Your daughter understands she has your unconditional love, so teach her thoughtfully for a positive outcome. You are everything to her. You are the center of her world. Do not take her words to heart. She is testing you, which is why you need to teach her with love. Help her to pass her test!

# 3

# Communication

## Introduction: What Are You Really Saying?

How you communicate to your child will determine how much information he will obtain or retain. Your communication can actually determine how, if, and when he will respond. Unclear communication is an underlying cause of why so many children do not do what they are told or unnecessarily melt down into a tantrum. Imagine eliminating tantrums and getting your child to do what you say when you say it. No matter what your child's age, you can absolutely connect and communicate so your child will respond. This chapter provides information on verbal communication, word usage, nonverbal communication, as well as the power of a physical touch to provide positive reinforcement.

## What We Say and What They Hear May Be Two Different Things

What you say, how you say it, the way you use your words, your sentence structure, your tone of voice, as well as the words you choose will absolutely determine how your child interprets the importance of your message. Sending a clear message requires a clear statement, such as "It's time to start your homework now" or "It's time to clean up your toys now." Parents often ask their child to do things, using the words "okay" or "please," which indicate a request rather than a directive. Requests may or may not be fulfilled. Requests are confusing for children because they interpret that they have an option. However, when a child misinterprets a directive as a request and does not comply, parents become angry, feeling their child is misbehaving. Learn to say what you mean and mean what you say, but do not say it mean.

Sometimes, a message is delivered in the form of a threat, such as, "If you don't finish your dinner, then you can't have dessert." "If you don't … then you can't" is a threat, although you may not have thought of it as such. Many parents threaten without realizing it. Threatening makes the recipient (your child) defensive. Sometimes a child will retaliate by responding with an aggressive behavior or a temper tantrum, or sometimes he will reply, "I don't care." In either case, you won't achieve the desired result, which was for your child to do something, for example, eat dinner. Read how to turn threats into motivational decisions by using "when and then" statements.

Sandwiching your language is very effective when providing information that your child may not want to hear. Read how to provide three simple sentences with positive reinforcers and a directive slipped in the middle of the sandwich. The less information you provide at one time, the easier it is for your child to digest!

## Messaging with Impact

Nonverbal communication occurs in households every day, sending a variety of messages. You may not even realize the negative nonverbal messages you send but then wonder why your child rolls his eyes or slams a door. Body language, eye rolling, crossed arms, loud sighs, slamming of a door, or slamming down an object is a form of communication and teaches your child to do the same. Unspoken, nonverbal communication can also provide positive reinforcement when you give a smile, a wink, or two thumbs-up. Even more powerful is your physical presence, when you get up and go over to your child to touch him as you are telling him what a nice job (of sharing or cleaning up) he is doing. You teach your child through your actions. He listens to you, watches you, and focuses on your facial expressions. He hears you laugh, watches you cry, listens to you sigh, watches how you interact with family and friends, and he waits to feel your gentle touch of approval. These are just some of the many ways you communicate with your child whenever he is near. Your child can learn how to express his feelings with words rather than aggressive actions, as everything you do teaches him how to communicate, behave, and respond. This chapter provides powerful information with simple strategies to strengthen whole family communication, making it easy to connect closely.

How you communicate with your child directly impacts how he will respond. Change your language from a request into a clear directive in order to send a clear message. There's no need to get frustrated, yell, or repeat yourself. Simply go to your child ( yes, get up and go), bend down to make a connective, gentle touch, and then give a clear directive, such as, "It's time to ..." Connecting both physically and verbally ensures that your child will understand your message.

While giving your directive, it is important to eliminate words that invite negotiation, such as "okay." For example:

- "Get up to bed now, okay?"
- "Get your homework done, okay?"
- "Clean up your toys, okay?"

Asking your child to go to bed, start homework, or clean up toys may end with confrontation simply because of how it was presented. Children sense reluctance or hesitation, which they interpret as a lack of parental control. That is often when a child will take control by ignoring the request or having a tantrum to distract and wear his parent down until she gives in.

It is also important to speak in "dos" instead of "don'ts."[22] For example:

- "Don't put your feet on the couch."
- "Don't run through the house."
- "Don't leave your dishes on the table."

Young children rely on their experiences to visualize what is being said to them. "Don't" is an abstract word, and children cannot visualize it. They hear a raised voice, which they interpret as yelling, and then they will visualize feet, run, or dishes and miss the importance of message. Communicate clearly to tell your child what you do want. Say "Feet go on the floor" as you walk by and touch his legs. Then, of course, give verbal praise with a gentle touch as an immediate reward for following directions. Although it can be difficult to learn to speak in "dos," when you make the effort, you'll soon see cooperative results with your child!

The following are four little words to eliminate from your vocabulary when giving a directive:

---

22  *The Incredible Years*, 74.

- **Ask and Please.** "How many times do I have to ask you to please get your feet off the couch?" Parents often use the word "please" to model manners, hoping their child will learn through example of a mannerly request. "Please" implies that you are asking. Eliminate the words "ask" and "please" unless you are making a request.
- **Let's.** "Let's get up to bed now … Let's get those toys cleaned up!" That word leaves room for negotiation. Replace it with a clear directive, such as, "It's time to …" and emphasize your directive with a touch.
- **We.** Eliminate the word "we" when correcting a misbehavior, as in "We don't hit!" Think about it. We didn't hit. Your child hit. Keep the focus on your child and replace "we" with "you." "You may not hit" sends a clear, strong message.

Remember that you will achieve better results when giving your child an important message if you get up and go, keep it short, be very clear, make a connective touch, and watch your language!

I worked with a mom who said her six-year-old had worn her down to tears. She said he was demanding and constantly negotiating. She said he was relentless with questions and accusations and always full of hurtful words when she attempted to set boundaries. She said he could go on for hours. I asked how she handled it, and she said she tried to convince him to stop, telling him that he was wrong or rude. I said, "Don't dance with him." She looked at me as if I were crazy. Then I said, "As a matter of fact, don't even go to the party!" Have you ever heard the expression that it takes two to tango? I asked her what would happen if she set a boundary for her child and then walked away rather than stay and negotiate. She replied that he would yell or cry and try to reengage with her. I encouraged her to try a new strategy and assured her that it would get easier as she consistently provided the same response without dancing.

I told her about a similar situation with a mom of a four-year-old who did learn to set boundaries. When she initially said no, her son knocked over the ficus tree in their living room. Unfortunately, she reacted and reengaged by screaming about the mess and the broken branches on the tree. Her son screamed, saying she was mean and it was all her fault because she yelled at him. She screamed right back at him, saying he was in big trouble and would have privileges taken away. Back and forth they argued. Perfect. That was exactly what her child was looking for, a dance partner! She had just trained her child that, if he wanted her attention after she said no, he should do something very dramatic. I suggested she not dance. She shouldn't even look at him as he went through the motions of his tantrum. He needed to learn two important pieces of information: that his behavior was unacceptable and she was there for him whenever he was ready to apologize. Unconditional love helps a child self-regulate, de-escalate, and apologize.

As the story goes, the next time she set a boundary, her son knocked over the tree and a chair! He had escalated his behavior, as I told her he might. This time, she ignored the upturned tree and the toppled chair and left the room. He followed her, screaming and pulling at her pant leg. She bent down, touched him with some gentle pressure, and said that, when he was quiet, then he could come to her. She took deep breaths, busied herself with household tasks, and ignored his attempts to invite her to his party. When her son came to her exhausted, she modeled the exact apology for his exact behavior, which included his hurtful words and throwing the tree and the chair. When he did apologize, she accepted without a lecture, hugged him, and got out the dustpan to help him clean up his mess. She wanted him to learn she would not negotiate. She wanted him to learn boundaries and the rules of life. She wanted to teach him that he would have to be responsible for his actions. So she held the dustpan while he swept in the dirt.

When I told that story to the mom of the six-year-old, she understood what I meant when I said, "Don't dance." She telephoned me several days later to say that her son exploded when she set a boundary. She put up her hand to signal a stop sign and walked down to the basement to fold laundry. She remained calm and repeated to herself, "Don't dance. Don't even go to the party." It worked because he had no audience. He de-escalated, went to his room, tore his sheets off his bed, and sat on his floor. He came to her later and apologized. She asked what he was apologizing for, and he said for yelling and not listening. She hugged him and said she was glad he apologized, never remarking on his torn-up bed. He fixed his sheets at bedtime and climbed in.

When a child sees that he has no audience, no one to dance with, and no party, he will learn to listen and come to understand that no means no.

Say what you mean and mean what you say, but don't say it mean! That one very powerful phrase suggests we be clear, consistent, and thoughtful with what we say and how we say it. Parents have the opportunity to be the most amazing teachers, providing their child with safe ways to learn life lessons. Teaching with threats or bribery are ineffective options because they teach the wrong lesson. Sometimes a parent is not even aware of the threatening, overpowering behaviors that intimidate or frighten his child. When parents are positive, offering help or motivation, they will achieve better results. Tell your child what you do want him to do and offer motivation or your help instead of a threat.

The dictionary defines a threat as a declaration of intent to punish or hurt. Without realizing it, parents threaten children in an effort to motivate them:

- "If you don't eat your dinner, you can't have dessert."
- "If you don't clean up, I'm throwing out your toys."
- "If you don't do your homework, you can't watch TV."

Some children reply, "I don't even want to watch TV!" Then that parent has lost his leverage. At that point, parents may find themselves trying to convince their child that, yes, they really do want to watch TV because it's his favorite show. Some parents begin to beg or even bribe their child. What a mess!

It's simple enough to change your language from "If you don't, then you can't" to "When you do, then you can!" Send a message that you expect it to happen, remove the threat, and provide a motivation. Now, that's parenting! Always think about the message you are sending. When you threaten, you are only a "power over" parent, one who says, "You do it because I said so because I will punish you." It seems simple enough. Either do what you are told or be punished! However, teaching a child is not quite that simple. Think about the lesson you are teaching. A child needs to learn to do what he is told, not out of fear but out of respect for following your rules. Threats don't teach a lesson. They intimidate and teach fear.

Much of the time, parents don't follow through with their threats because, after they have made them, they realize they were unrealistic, overstated, or unnecessary. And once a child learns that his parent doesn't follow through with threats, he has no motivation to obey, so he doesn't do what he is told. When a child does not do what he is told, the negative cycle continues. We yell and threaten again, and our parental gift of teaching a lesson is long gone. Change your threat, "If you don't (finish your dinner) then you can't (have any dessert)" to a positive statement with an incentive, "When you do finish your dinner, then you may have this fabulous little dessert I made just for you!"

We know that children learn what they live. If a parent threatens, his child will learn to threaten others. Instead, teach your child with respect by teaching him to learn to do the right thing for the right reason. Be firm, be consistent, be positive, and eliminate threats. When your child complies, let him know how proud you are that he made a good choice by doing what he was told. Make a gentle, connective touch while giving your directive, and your effectiveness will increase without threats. If you do find yourself yelling or threatening, take a breath, and remember you are your child's most important teacher.

"Get up and go!" is a powerful strategy to implement when you want to send an important message to your child. Your physical presence with a connective touch is a very powerful yet quiet message. It's like magic. So whether you want to increase or decrease a behavior, just add a little "get up and go!" Families spend so much of their time yelling from another room, from another floor of the house, or across the backyard. They yell to come to dinner, they yell that there's a phone call, they yell to come clean up, they yell for their kids to stop fighting, and they yell for their kids to stop yelling! When parents take the time to walk over to their child and touch him as they are speaking, they provide multisensory communication. The child can then feel his parent's mood and message by how softly or firmly he is touched. When parents couple that with verbal praise or redirection, their child's brain integrates the message through both senses. The benefit of sending a multisensory message is that a child is much more likely to respond immediately because a clear message of high importance has been given through touch. It is such a simple technique, yet way too often, parents don't take the time to get off the couch and make it happen.

When it is dinnertime, get up and go to your child, give a gentle touch, and tell him his dinner is waiting. Eliminate yelling from room to room, and eliminate yelling, "How many times do I have call you for dinner?" Instead, say it with a touch. When he comes to the table, get up and go to him, saying you are proud of him for coming when he was called. When your child is eating with nice manners, get up and go across the table, and give a kiss on the head or touch on his shoulder, remarking about how much you love his manners when he chews with his mouth closed. Too many times we expect or even demand a behavior but don't think to provide recognition when the effort is made.

When it is time to do homework, get up and go to your child, touching him gently and saying, "It's time for you to do your homework. I've cleared a spot for you at the kitchen table, so I can help you." While he is doing his homework, reach over and acknowledge how hard he is working.

When you see your child pushing another child, get up and go to your child, bend down, and hold firmly on his shoulder, saying, "You may not push!" Then go to the recipient and offer comfort, support, or attention. Your child will want your attention. At which point, you can help him to apologize for hitting, explaining that hitting really hurts.

When your child is frustrated or accelerating into a tantrum because he can't get his shoes on, get up and go to him, touch him gently on the shoulder, and say, "If you need help, I can help you." That close touch with an offer of help is more effective than calling from across the room, "Hurry up and get your shoes on, or we will be late!"

When you see your child sharing, get up and go, bend down, and give a gentle touch on his head or shoulder, remarking, "I just love to watch you share." Too often we focus on and punish for negative behavior rather than recognize all the positive behaviors that a young child displays.

You will have greater success with a multisensory approach,[23] no matter what you are trying to communicate to your child. The strategy is simple, and the results are remarkable!

## Be Mindful of Your Message

I often visit classrooms with a behavior management plan in place. Most classrooms have behavior plans because children respond well and work hard whenever there is a reward. Young children need extrinsic rewards (tangible prizes) as motivators, but as they grow, they can be transitioned to intrinsic (feel good) rewards, such as time with us. Whether you are a classroom teacher or parent at home, a behavior plan with clear expectations, rewards, and privileges can provide the motivation that children need to succeed. All of us work better or have a better day when someone takes a moment to tell us that our work is meaningful or we have done a good job. Children are learning the ropes of life and need incentives with tremendous encouragement, even more so than adults do. Most classroom incentives can be easily implemented in your own home. Find out which motivators your child's teacher is using, and see if they fit with your parenting style.

When I taught disabled teenagers, I copied dollar bills onto green paper and endorsed my name on each bill, turning them into "Boggia Bucks," which students earned for the three As: attempts, achievements, and acts of kindness. Each Friday was shopping day, although students could earn a Bonus Buck if they saved their money and did not buy on impulse. At that time, I was slowly cleaning out my home, so radios, portable CD players, alarm clocks, and music CDs from my children filled

---

23 *The Worried Child*, 108.

my Friday Store. Students throughout the school admired the store. They often stopped by to tell me that they did something wonderful to see if I would reward them with some "Boggia Bucks," which I did. I felt that every act of kindness or attempt to achieve or succeed on a test deserved recognition. It was a complete success for everyone as I emptied my home and the students earned as they learned.

Classroom behavioral plans have been in place forever. I remember growing up and earning lunch with the principal as the highest of rewards. I also earned lunch with my teacher in kindergarten. There were always motivators. Today, I see lots of school systems using green cards for good behavior, or a child may be given a different colored card as a warning. A marble jar has been around for years, where the entire class works (by being quiet or kind) toward a common goal (of a class party). Stickers are always favored among younger children. For more ideas on how to improve your child's social or emotional functioning in your home or at school, visit my informational, educational website at www.yourperfectchild.com.

I had the opportunity to observe a class where a beautiful doghouse was constructed on the bulletin board and every student had his name printed on a dog bone. Each time a child distracted the class, forgot an assignment, or talked out of turn, he was directed to move his bone up the path toward the doghouse. I watched as one little boy whispered, "I'm almost in the doghouse!" My first instinct was to laugh, thinking that children say the funniest things! However, I realized that "in the doghouse" is an abstract concept, and this child was playing a game of moving his dog bone toward the end goal of getting into the doghouse. Talking to his neighbor earned him another move with his bone, and he called out, "I'm almost in the doghouse!" The teacher responded, "Yes, you are, and that is not something you should be proud of!" She had no idea that he didn't understand her rules that he was, in fact, being punished while he thought he was winning.

We know that children are tactile, concrete, hands-on learners. Children have learned to play board games understanding the goal is to move their piece toward the end. The other missing piece to this game is that "in the doghouse" is a negative, abstract concept, and children do not start to develop abstract thinking until around age six or seven. Some of those young children who were just learning to think outside the box did not understand the message or consequence, and there were not any rewards.

So, the lesson of the day is to be careful what you teach and how you teach it. Be careful which incentives you provide, and determine if they are age-appropriate. Provide your child with lots of praise and incentives, both intrinsic and extrinsic, to help him work toward a goal with success.

## Keep Conversations Simple by Making Sandwiches

When parents speak, their child will often tune out or turn off long before the point is made. Adults have a tendency to over talk, explain too much, or give much more information than their young child is even able to process. I recall a funny story of a five-year-old who asked where babies came from. His mom painfully explained some basic biology as her child squirmed and fidgeted. The mom was careful with her wording, but the explanation was involved. At the end of the explanation, his mom said, "So, do you understand where babies come from?" Her child said, "I don't really know because my friend said he came from the hospital!" When teaching a child, providing information, or giving a directive, keep it simple in three sentences or fewer. Young children are able to process information with success when it is simple and clear.

Sometimes, parents send a backdoor directive, a roundabout message. Instead of stating, "It's time to get your PJs on and get ready for bed," a parent might say, "It's time to start to think about going to bed now because we know how cranky you can get when you haven't had enough sleep, and then you will be miserable tomorrow. So I think it might be a good idea if you start to change into your PJs." Perhaps parents say way too much because they fear their child will complain when he is directly told to get ready for bed. A favorite quote of mine is, "It's not what you say but how you say it." I am a very firm believer in sending a clear message with a connective physical touch to guide a multisensory message that is clearly communicated.

I have educated many parents on the skill of sandwiching their message, making the information more palatable for a child to process and digest. I worked with a family with a six-year-old who became easily frustrated and either whined loudly or broke down into a loud cry when he didn't get what he wanted. His mom had been telling him to stop whining for quite some time, but that did not change his behavior. So, I suggested she sandwich her message by following these steps:

1. Get up and go to him, and make a gentle connective touch.

2. Layer the sandwich. Offer the bottom piece of bread by saying, "I can tell that you are really upset." When a child feels that others are empathetic, it often defuses some heightened emotions.

3. Provide the precise message you want to send, the meat of the sandwich. "I'd like to be able to help you, but I can't understand you when you are whining or screaming."

4. Finish your sandwich with a wonderful, soft piece of fresh bread. Tell your child that, when he comes to you quietly and is able to whisper, then you will be able to help him. Follow up with a little loving touch on his face or head, and walk away. Initially, this may be difficult to do, but with practice and consistency, you will soon have noticeable success.

Please note that telling a child to calm down is not a clear message. Calm is abstract. Children will scream, "I am calm!" It is better to suggest that, when he can whisper to you, then you'll be able to understand what he wants. It may take a little practice, but everyone loves a good sandwich.

## Teach and Communicate Using Secret Codes

Thumbs-up and high fives aren't the only ways to show a job well done. There are endless nonverbal hand signs, as well as quick verbal cues, that express excitement, encouragement, and positive communication. While playing a competitive game of dominoes with neighbors, the men developed a knuckle knock with each winning round. They seemed to form a bond of camaraderie and support with their connection, and they went on to win the game! Children can be easily excited with secret codes and love to be included in secrets. They love little winks or two thumbs-up for a job well done.

While raising my children, when I made an absolute promise, my daughter would ask, "Mom, do you thumb and pinkie swear to it?" I did not promise often, but when I did, I kept my word. If I were sure I could deliver the promise, I would thumb and pinkie swear by connecting our thumbs and pinkie fingers in a sort of handshake and then give each other a wink. She is now twenty-three, but I am certain that, if I promised her something even today, she would ask if I would thumb and pinkie swear to it.

When I taught disabled teenagers, developing sign language and secret codes was a very effective form of positive classroom management.

Although classes were small with only twelve or thirteen students, each student needed individualized attention all day long. I was able to connect with each student by using a lot of secret, individualized codes that did not disrupt the class or embarrass any student with public redirection or humiliation.

The following are some easy secret tips to try in your home.

- From a distance, a simple double thumbs-up provides visual reinforcement. Also, matching up your thumb to meet your child's thumb with the sound of a sizzle implies that he is focused and on fire!

- For those children who have a difficult time keeping their hands to themselves, you can teach the HIP code. Hit your side hip and say "HIP," teaching the acronym for "hands in pockets." You may be surprised to see your child hurry in an attempt to be first to get his hands in his pockets. Rather than repeat, "Keep your hands to yourself" or "Stop touching everyone," a quick HIP can be a fun reminder. It eliminates identifying a specific child or humiliating a child in public while still meeting the goal of teaching personal space. You can transition from providing multisensory cues (verbalizing HIP while hitting your hip) to just one cue, deciding whether a verbal or visual cue is more effective for your child.

- CC stands for "common courtesy." When children all rush to be first, they can be rude and impatient, pushing, shoving, or knocking each other out of the way through a doorway, just to be first to the table or car. A quick, verbal reminder of "Stop! CC!" does not admonish anyone or decrease enthusiasm. It just serves as a reminder to be thoughtful and courteous while making it very clear that you are watching.

Many parents struggle with a child who walks into a bedroom or bathroom without knocking. Oftentimes, children often do not understand the need for privacy and simply need to be taught. Rather than repeating yourself over and over, place a simple octagonal red paper with the word "stop" written on it as a visual reminder on specific doors. Teach your child the rhyming words "stop and knock," practice with him often, and then praise him when he does it.

The very effective Two Tap is described in the Building Skills chapter, which provides a child with his own code to let a parent know that he wants his attention. A child can be successfully taught to approach an adult and ask for help rather than be scolded for interrupting.

Teaching expectations through multisensory communication codes (visual, auditory, and tactile) is much more effective than yelling or issuing constant ineffective reminders, producing rapid, positive results. When learning is fun (when it becomes a game), children are most always ready and willing to play!

## Getting More Than a Yes or No Answer

Getting information from a child can sometimes be very difficult, as young children are concrete thinkers. They speak in black and white, such as good or bad or yes or no. Parents can easily learn to elicit information from a young child, helping that child to respond with more than a one-word answer. How a question is asked may determine how a child will respond. A mom of an eight-year-old said she couldn't get much out of her son when he came home from school. She said a typical conversation would be:

"How was your day?"
"Good."
"Great! How was your test?"
"Fine."
"Did you like your lunch?"
"Yep."
"Do you have homework?"
"Nope."

I suggested that mom ask questions that require more than a one-word answer. Questions that elicit a different response might include: What game did you play in gym today? What was the toughest question on your social studies test this morning? Who did you play with at recess?

Try using as many "wh" questions as possible (who, what, when, where, or why do you think). "Wh" questions generally require more than a one-word response and can ignite a whole conversation. It is so important to teach children how to communicate so they learn to become comfortable with expressing their feelings or anything else that is going on in their lives. As they grow, their lives will become so much more complicated, and although they may not think it necessary, they obviously do need guidance, input, and boundaries as their decision making skills are immature and require tremendous scaffolding. With each day, a child learns how to navigate through life, but he may not seek help until his ship sails way off course. Good communication is an excellent anchor.

Evenings and bedtime can be a wonderful time to find out what your child is thinking, who his friends are, or how successful he was in school. Evenings are often a time when children are ready to decompress and talk to their parents, as proven by the child who needs just one more glass of water or has just one more question to ask before bed. Parents, however, are generally focused on rushing through dinner, finishing homework to start baths, and getting everyone to bed without a struggle. Change your focus and develop a mind-set to dedicate much of your evening to your child. He will sense that he has your attention and will be able to relax enough to talk his way into bed, closing out another day with his mom or dad. After story time and dimmed lights, ask three questions to initiate conversation that highlight the events of the day. Clarify concerns, and resolve insecurities or uncertainties. Ask the following: What was the best thing that happened to you today? What was the worst thing that happened today? What are you looking forward to tomorrow? That is a form on sandwiching your language, as you start with something positive, address concerns in the middle, and end with a positive thought or question. Sandwiching your questions is also great for dinner conversation.[24]

Other questions that can increase communication and self-confidence might be the following: What was the nicest thing you did for someone today? How do you think you can make tomorrow a better day? If you have these quiet conversations when your child is in bed, tucked in safely, he may become more willing to open up, providing valuable information that might otherwise be missed.

While my three children were growing up, I spent my evenings with each of them, individually reading and then talking quietly until they had wound down and each felt safe, secure, and ready to sleep. I put each child to bed, one at a time, as the other two read to themselves waiting for me. I did not know much about the latest TV programs, but I learned a great deal about what my three children were thinking and how they were handling situations. I helped them through many concerns that I would not have known about until after the fact, simply because bedtime was the right time for them to communicate. I followed their lead, their need to talk before drifting off. It made bedtime a very valuable time for all of us. I was able to help them process their day and ready themselves for tomorrow. My bedtime routine with my three children continues to pay off, as they

---

24  *Thinking Parent, Thinking Child*, 33.

continue to communicate with me about their young adult lives, their work, their politics, and their passions. What more could a parent want?

# Dear Diana

*Rude Comments and Hurtful Words*

Dear Diana, I recently overheard my three-and-a-half-year-old say to his grandma, "You're old and fat!" To him, all adults are old, but she is also substantially overweight. How do I explain to him that, even though these things may be true, it's rude and mean to call someone fat? His grandma just laughed it off at the time, unknowingly encouraging those types of comments. He has stated his opinion about our neighbors as well. "He's a mean old dad!" and "They're just old people!" I'm not getting the concept through to him. Instead, I just hear, "But she is fat."

Dear Mom, It might be helpful to identify the source of some of these comments. He may be learning to be critical from a children's movie or neighborhood kids. Rather than responding to him after he has used hurtful words, set him up for success by teaching, explaining, and helping him to apologize. Children learn best by doing, so help him to apologize and teach him what is expected.

Speak to your son privately when you have his full attention. Explain all of the exact words that are hurtful, those that may not be used, including the following: fat, old, and mean. Do this outside of the event, while sitting at the kitchen table with a bowl of popcorn, explaining the new rules. Do not wait for it to happen again. He may think it is funny to use those words because, as you stated, he has gotten the response of laughter, although it was probably uncomfortable, nervous laughter. Children have difficulty interpreting unclear communication. The message he may have received was that people thought he was funny when he used those words. Be very clear with your expectations. Let him know that, if he makes a mistake and does say hurtful things to anyone, you will let him know on the spot and help him to apologize to that person immediately. If you hear about it after the fact, take him immediately to apologize. He will undoubtedly be resistant as well as uncomfortable, but apologizing is a natural consequence.

The purpose of an apology is to teach, not to humiliate or embarrass. Even at his age, he will be taking responsibility for his actions, which are his words. Taking responsibility will help him to understand, internalize, and self-regulate. He may be extremely hesitant, but when you help him to walk over to say, "I'm sorry for saying you're fat" or "I'm sorry for what I said," he will learn quickly in an appropriate setting. If your son refuses to speak or apologize, bend down to his level, and say it for him, "Johnny is having a hard time apologizing, but he wants you to know that he is sorry for what he said." It is helpful if the adult on the receiving end accepts the apology rather than accept with a lecture, such as "Well, I hope you don't say that ever again because …" A lecture is a turnoff. The true lesson has already been taught through the actual experience of the apology. Perhaps he can draw a picture, present some garden flowers, or offer an act of kindness as a means of apologizing. When your son does learn to apologize, be sure to provide positive reinforcement, telling him, "That may have been hard, but I am proud of you for apologizing." Apologies are not innate; they are learned. Children need to be taught how to apologize.

A parent's response to his child's behavior will often determine how his child will behave. Parents have asked, "If my child bites, should I bite him back to teach him how it feels?" Absolutely not! We are their role models. It is a mixed message to say "Don't bite!" and then bite a child to teach a lesson or say "Don't hit!" while spanking. Instead, teach through positive experiences and consistent reinforcement. Humiliation, criticism, and embarrassment diminish self-esteem and escalate inappropriate behavior. Parents may hesitate to correct their child in public because they are concerned about escalating the situation into an uncontrollable, embarrassing backlash or temper tantrum. It is helpful to remember that these experiences are as valuable as those in a preschool classroom. The world is your child's training ground. While teaching your child, take a breath, and face a tantrum as another opportunity to refine your parenting skills in public. Other parents will watch how you handle the situation and admire your follow-through.

# Dear Diana

*Repeating Questions*

$\mathcal{D}$ear $\mathcal{D}$iana, I heard you speak at my daughter's preschool and really enjoyed your presentation. We have been working hard to implement the consistent routines that you recommended, and they are working wonderfully! However, I have a four-year-old who, after asking a question and receiving an answer, continues to ask the same question. Sometimes, the answer may be, "Yes, but in a few minutes," but she will continue to ask. I realize that, at some point, I must have given in for her to believe that she'll get what she wants if she asks again. I know my first step is to be consistent, but how else should I handle the situation? I'm not sure if it warrants a time-out. What would you suggest? Mom of Questions and Answers

Dear Mom of Questions and Answers, Answering your daughter's repetitive questions will need to be your new area of focus, as it sounds like you have learned to be successful with consistency in routines. Now, it is time to become consistent with your communication as well. You may be responding differently with your words as well as your content, so your daughter feels there is wiggle room to get you to change your mind. Your voice (lower or higher intonation as well as volume level) will send a message of confidence or your expectation of her pushback. Inconsistencies, such as sticking to what you say 80 percent of the time with a 20 percent chance of changing your mind, will teach her to negotiate harder, beg for longer periods, and tantrum louder, having learned that she just might be successful in wearing you down.

As a parent, I totally understand about giving in, feeling worn out, or simply saying, "Okay, just this once." However, as both a parent and an educator, I know that is ineffective because children see our change of heart as their success (a reward) for their hard work (a tantrum). Children need boundaries. They need to know what to expect, and they need to be able to rely on your answer remaining the same.

You wrote that your daughter continues to ask again and again. She does this because you have changed your answer in the past. She asks to find out if you will change your answer again. A time-out is not warranted because she is not misbehaving. She is testing communication. Change your communication to help her change her behavior.

The following are suggestions to eliminate continuous questions:

- Before you answer your daughter, decide, "What is my answer?" Learn to say, "I'll think about it and let you know after breakfast." Once you give an answer, you must stick to it, as you are training her to accept that boundary.

- Decide on the language you will always use, so you train her ear to hear, "Yes, when you finish your dinner, then you may have ice cream." Training her to listen for your answer is the first step. When you start your answer with "when," she will learn to listen for the "then."

- Give a benchmark time frame when responding. Children are concrete thinkers, so abstract answers such as "maybe later," "in a few minutes," "not right now," or "probably tomorrow" leave a parent open for continuous questioning. For a child, five minutes is later. Use phrases including,
  - "Yes, you may. After lunch."
  - "When it is dark."
  - "After our company leaves."
  - "Yes, when you wake up tomorrow."

When you say "tomorrow," take her to the calendar and let her draw something on tomorrow to represent the activity for tomorrow.

- Set a timer if you need to identify a specific time (2:30). Place the timer where she can watch the minutes tick away to help her accept and internalize your answer.

- Be mindful of your tone of voice and your consistent wording. Speak with confidence, not annoyance.

- Do not show frustration or anger with her repetitive questions. Simply repeat your exact prior response, "Yes, after breakfast." Your frustration may be the fuel she's looking for, so her continuous questions have become misbehavior rather than a lack of clear communication.

How a parent communicates and responds in nearly every situation will determine a child's success. Mindful communication, patience, and your understanding that you are his role model will give you the results you are looking for.

# Dear Diana

*My Daughter, the Complainer*

Dear Diana, I am the mother of two girls, ages five and seven. I have learned many strategies that have improved our overall family life from your column. However, we have a continuous problem with our seven-year-old, who complains about absolutely everything. She is never happy or satisfied. We've actually nicknamed her "Carley the Complainer." She merely tolerates her sister. They don't have a good relationship. Carley seems to feel that her younger sister gets more attention. Honestly, her younger sister is more enjoyable to be around, so people are naturally drawn to her. We constantly tell her we love her, but she doesn't seem to believe it. Now when Carley gets angry, she overeats, and she is gaining weight. Her complaints affect our whole family as we try to please her or explain our decisions to her. I'm open to any suggestions because what we're doing is not working. Thanks, Carley's Mom

Dear Carley's Mom, Over time, you can minimize Carley's complaints and change how she feels about things by incorporating some new, positive strategies. It is important to know that even an occasional reference to her nickname, "Carley the Complainer," is unproductive as well as hurtful to her development because, as long as she is labeled, she will continue to be angry, complain, and live up to her negative nickname. Carley has learned to get your attention by complaining. That is her way of expressing her feelings that things are unfair and she feels less loved. You have said that she always seems unhappy. Her unhappiness may be the root of her complaints. Complaints are her way of getting your (negative) attention. Children thrive on parent's attention, negative or positive. Taking the time to find out why she is unhappy may resolve many of the issues that might otherwise become complaints. Ask her questions. You do not need to agree with her, justify your actions, or convince her to feel different. Just let her know that she is being heard. Respond with, "I'm sorry you feel that way" or "What do you think you can do to change that?" Show her how much you love her by making extra time for her. Structured activities that include both girls will improve their sibling relationship.

It is important to remember that a child's perception is her reality. If she perceives and believes that her sister is better loved, then that is her reality. If she does feel less loved, simply telling her you love her will not change her attitude. You need to find ways to make her feel your love. If you continue to become angry or frustrated with her complaints, you will continue to get from her what you are getting now. Remember, nothing changes if nothing changes. You need to change your patterns in order to change her patterns. When Carley complains, touch her gently so she knows you heard her. With kindness and empathy, tell her you are sorry she is unhappy with the decision, and move on. Stay in control. Redirect her to another conversation or activity. It is important not to respond to her complaints, which would train her to continue. Do not defend because that ignites negotiation and provides the opportunity for further argument. Responding to her specific complaints is not productive because it empowers her as a complainer.

Do not focus on Carley's overeating, as that can become a power struggle with medical complications. Speak with your pediatrician, and remove the junk food from your home. Her emotional eating is her way of filling up those empty spaces inside. Instead, focus on filling those places with love, confidence, and positive praise for all she does well. As her self-confidence rises, her need to satisfy herself with food should diminish. Increase her physical activity without bringing attention to it. Invite her on a bike ride or a race up the stairs. You can turn her life around if you make it your focus. How lucky she is to have you for her mom!

4

# Building Skills

## Introduction: You Can Teach Anything

There are so many ways to improve your child's behavior, but simply expecting or telling your child to behave is not going to make it happen. Children need to be taught over and over by example with multisensory communication, consistency, and love. Within each article in this chapter, positive strategies are included to teach new, desired skills to set up your child for success. Additionally, each of the following articles offers information regarding the effectiveness of teaching outside of the moment.

Distressing, embarrassing behaviors can be eliminated and replaced with thoughtful, well-mannered behaviors. When parents see the same behavior reoccurring over and over again, they often lose patience or yell out of frustration. If you have been unable to change a behavior by telling or yelling, try some of the positive teaching strategies in this chapter. The misbehavior of the moment always needs to be immediately addressed with a correction, but in order to change that misbehavior, to teach a new skill, or to eliminate an unwanted behavior, you will be most effective when you teach outside of the event. Read how to be more successful at another time when you are able to teach and your child is able to hear and learn. Determine a replacement behavior you want, and then provide a positive training ground for practice, the scaffolding for successful skill building. You can teach or retrain your child by providing the information he needs through multisensory communication and modeling.

The things we pay attention to will definitely continue or increase, depending on the amount or type of attention we provide. It is basic

60

human nature. Think about a compliment you have recently received and how it made you feel. Did your self-confidence rise? Did you repeat that behavior again because you were complimented? If someone said you looked absolutely great in a particular pair of black slacks, you would probably wear them often, perhaps every day with a different shirt, blouse, or sweater. The top would change, but the pants would remain because you received a powerful compliment. Providing continuous, positive reinforcement to your child (for the exact behavior) will result in improved behaviors.

In this chapter, you can read about the successful steps to teach your child to hold your hand in public. Read how to teach your child to help you shop at the market instead of running through aisles, begging for cookies and candy. Read about the incremental training steps to use to teach your child to wait with patience while you are on the phone. Another article offers information on how to change your response to minimize or eliminate complaining or whining. Read how to teach table manners with ease, as you turn dinnertime into a family restaurant game. Another article offers training for the Two Tap, so that with a few simple, repetitive steps, you can teach your child to say, "Excuse me" instead of interrupting. And read about teaching apologies for mistakes or lies, so you will become comfortable to tell the truth. Any behavior can be changed, just as any child can be taught the skills we want him to have. The determining factors for success are how and when they are taught.

## Build Skills, Develop Independence, and Raise Self-Esteem

You can raise your child's self-esteem, starting today. Children with high self-esteem display fewer misbehaviors. They are higher academic achievers, and they develop strong, healthy peer relationships. They are confident problem solvers. Self-esteem is built from successful experiences. Children experience success when they try, do, and accomplish new things. They learn quickly with hands-on doing, and they love to help, as evidenced by the many popular child-sized toys such as vacuums, lawn mowers, shopping carts, and kitchen sets. Each time a child tries, does, and is successful in learning a new skill, his self-confidence soars. Unfortunately, as parents, we often do for our children what they can easily do for themselves, simply because we don't want them to feel burdened or often because it is so much easier or faster to do it ourselves. However, when parents do the work, it eliminates the opportunity for their child to build skills and develop independence. Encourage your child to help with daily chores, which will help him feel included, needed, and more a part of your family. Completing a simple task teaches a child that a job has a beginning and an end. It teaches responsibility, structure, multistep processing, and forward thinking (what should I do next?). Teaching small tasks, such as setting the table, sweeping crumbs from the floor with a small dustpan, or sorting colored socks will foster independence and build a sense of pride. Do not deprive your child by doing everything for him. Teach him.

The following are some fun ways for your child to help out, pitch in, and pick up:

- **Design a pickup pail.** Using markers and puffy stickers, help your child personalize a wash bucket with a handle. Each night, as part of your bedtime routine, walk through each room of the house with your child to pick up his belongings and pop them in his pail. Make it fun, and help him to put everything away. When your child learns he is responsible for putting his belongings away, he will be less likely to drop and go.

- **Create a helping hands job jar.** Cut out magazine pictures of items, including socks, clothing, towels, a hand vac or broom, and so forth. Trace your child's hand, cut out, and decorate a plastic container. Place magazine pictures inside, so your child can pick out a job each day (folding towels, sorting socks, vacuuming the car, and so forth). No peeking!

- **Create a place mat model.** Purchase inexpensive plastic place mats. Set a complete place setting on each place mat, and trace a plate, cup, fork, and so forth with permanent marker so your child has a model to set the table alone.

Remember to continually recognize all of your child's efforts and successes with verbal praise and a connective touch for high impact and increased self-esteem.

## No More Interrupting!

Teaching children to be patient is a challenge. Children feel that what they have to say is critically important and worthy of immediate attention. They interrupt when others are speaking, especially when their parent is on the phone. A parent may tend to ignore interruptions until they escalate, either in volume or behavior. That negative behavior will finally get a parent's attention. Remember that the things we pay attention to will continue, whether we provide negative or positive attention. So when you respond to a child's inappropriate interrupting or screaming, you are giving in and providing reinforcement for that behavior. If you continuously say, "Don't interrupt," that does not teach a change in behavior. Also, remember that nothing changes if nothing changes, which means that, if you do not like the way things are going, you need to change how you are teaching!

## *Do the Two Tap*

For a child who constantly interrupts, an effective approach to teaching patience and manners is to teach a replacement behavior for interrupting. Eliminate interrupting by teaching a little game I named the Two Tap, which teaches manners and patience. Children respond well because they become empowered with a strategy to attain their parent's immediate attention in a positive way. It is easily taught in two parts, about two weeks apart, for your child to be completely successful.

- **Part One: No More Interrupting.** Explain that, when your child wants something, he can come to you and tap you two times on the leg or arm, saying, "Excuse me." Model it for him, and role-play with him. Tap his arm two times, whisper the numbers "one, two," and then say out loud, "Excuse me!" Within days, your child will successfully implement the Two Tap if you immediately recognize, respond, and reward his efforts. Let him know what his rewards are:

  1. You will stop your conversation to hear his important message.

  2. You will respond with, "I am so proud of you for remembering the Two Tap."

  3. You will answer your child's question.

If your child interrupts you, forgetting to use the Two Tap, do not reprimand him with, "Don't interrupt! You should have done the Two Tap!" Instead, say less and do more. Model it for him by quietly taking his hand with your hand and tapping your leg twice, saying "One, two. Excuse me!" This teaching approach with physical engagement has a much bigger impact on his memory than negative reprimands.

- **Part Two: Learning to Wait.** After several weeks, when your child has consistently used a Two Tap, let him know you are so proud and you now are adding to the game. Tell him that, when he Two Taps, you will give him a signal. Hold up one finger, which means he needs to wait one minute, or hold up two fingers, which means, "I need a few minutes." Provide empathy, saying you understand how hard it can be to wait, but if he is able to wait, you will give him all of your attention when the time is up. It sounds simple because it is. Children want undivided attention, and this process provides exactly that.

*Reinforce Those Skills*

Each time your child does the Two Tap and waits patiently, it is critical that you respond to him as soon as possible, lavishing praise for remembering the game and his patience. Each time you mention the Two Tap, you are reinforcing that process in his memory with a positive emotional memory of receiving hugs, kisses, and all of your attention. This is child tested and parent proven over and over again. The Two Tap absolutely works!

## Stay with Me. Walk by My Side. Hold My Hand!

Stay with me! Walk by my side! So many parents have asked, "How can I get my child to stay with me when I am in a mall or a parking lot? He always runs away, and I'm afraid to take him anywhere!" Parents can easily train their child to walk beside them while holding hands, if they make the commitment to teach the lesson. Children love direction and boundaries, as it gives them a sense of security. When we do something over and over, we provide the security a child needs to learn with success.

*The Process*

Teach your child exactly what you want him to do, which is to hold your hand. Yelling at him while he is running through a mall will not teach him to walk by your side. Running after him will not teach the skill either, and running becomes extremely dangerous, as children often run further when someone is chasing them. To a child, running is simply a game. Teach the skill over and over until it becomes a natural part of your child's behavior. Take him for a walk every day to explore new things. Some days may require an umbrella; some days may require a coat. Some evenings, he can hold the flashlight, but every time you leave for your walk, he will be required to hold your hand. The following process will outline the steps you need to take:

- **Before you go.** Tell him that you will take him for a walk every day as long as he holds your hand. You can offer the choice of holding your belt loop or your finger, but he must remain connected. Teach him with the same repetitive procedure. This is his training, and time with you is his reward.

- **As you head out.** Ask if he remembers the rule. Remind him that you will continue on your walk as long as he holds your hand. If he drops your hand to pick up a leaf, quickly prompt him one time with a reminder that he needs to remain connected. If he tests you and breaks away running, pick him up and take him home, without discussion. It is not a punishment, but it is rather the consequence of his running. That is just the way it is. After many walks, he will learn that you will walk with him unless he runs away. When you follow through and pick him up to take him home, he will probably squirm or beg you for just one more chance. Your consistent response will determine his future success. It is so important to follow through, to pick him up and take him home, saying only, "I am so disappointed that you let go of my hand, and we had to end our walk." End the conversation, as there is no need to lecture. Actions speak louder than words.

- **The next day.** Begin the exact same way. Ask if he remembers the rule of holding hands. Remind him you will walk together as long as he holds on. Each day, you will be able to walk farther, and within a few weeks, you should have a child who willingly walks by your side.

- **Practice in the field.** Start in a safe, contained area, such as a grocery store. Set him up for success by shopping for only a few items. Provide the rules, check for understanding, and offer continuous verbal praise of how proud you are that he is holding your hand or the shopping cart handle. The more you praise him, the more successful he will be. If he runs in the store, he then loses the privilege of walking and must sit in the cart until your brief shopping trip is finished. Again, it is not a punishment; it is a consequence. Safety must always be given the highest priority.

Running is a game to many children, while it is an act of impulsivity for others. Setting expectations with layers of experience will provide the foundation a child needs to learn a new skill. The families I have worked with can now all take their children out and about because they were completely dedicated to a consistent training process. They played running games in the park and in the yard, so that running was given a time and a place. Their dedication to the process over several weeks gave them the peace of mind to know that their child will stay with them safely.

## Learning to Tell the Truth

Many children have difficulty taking ownership of their mistakes. They commonly deny wrongdoing or blame a sibling, which I refer to as the "Blame Game." Fairly typical responses from young children when they feel they are about to become admonished include:

- "I didn't do it."
- "It's his fault. He made me do it."
- "It wasn't my fault. He pushed me first."

Sometimes a child will tell a little fib. When asked to clarify, he will only find himself in the position of weaving a story around his little fib, which has become a grand lie. At that point, it is often too difficult for a child to admit he has lied for fear of the repercussions. Children can become comfortable with blaming or lying because it is easier than getting into trouble, and sometimes a lie sounds better than the truth. Many times, they do not get caught in their lies, so they learn to take a fifty-fifty chance of getting in trouble. Thomas Jefferson wrote, "He who permits himself to tell a lie once finds it much easier to do it a second and third time, till at length it becomes habitual."[25]

For a child, feeling safe enough to tell the truth is a wonderful feeling. Parents can make it easier for their child to tell the truth by teaching him that, if he makes a mistake, he can safely come back and tell the real story. Encouraging a child to come back without fear of punishment for lying provides safety and comfort, which helps him to be more successful in telling the truth time after time. Parents can locate many wonderful children's books to read together and later reinforce the topic with light conversation regarding the importance of trust and the truth. Providing

---

25 Thomas Jefferson letter, 1785.

a child with verbal praise and a gentle touch every time he is accurate or truthful will reinforce that desired behavior, which is the truth.

I met a family with a nine-year-old who told lies often throughout each day, many of which were insignificant pieces of information. Her parents were so concerned that she would become a habitual liar, so they began to feel the need to question everything she said. She was not trusted, and her word held no value. Nothing they tried made a difference, so they decided to try to break the cycle by teaching her the "come back." Using the phrase "come back" can make it less threatening for a child to implement the actual tool, the opportunity to return with the truth without getting into trouble. Shortly after her initial introduction of the come back, her dad questioned her about an obvious lie. He told her that it was very difficult to believe what she was saying, so perhaps she would like to think it over and use the come back. Not long after, she returned to say she was sorry because she had not told the truth. Her dad could have fallen into old patterns with admonishment and punishment for lying, but he didn't. He did not yell at her or question her as to why she lied. Instead, he remembered his goal, to have her learn to come back to him to tell him that she had made a mistake. He was delighted that she had chosen to come back and tell the truth. She had done so because she had been taught that she would be safe and not punished. He told her how proud he was that she came back to tell the truth, and together they figured out what her consequence should be for breaking the vase, which was to apologize to Grandma and then earn money to replace it. He asked her how she felt after telling the truth, and she said it felt good to be able to come back to him and be honest.

I warned her dad that, in certain situations, her first reaction may be to lie, as that has been her pattern for years and she has become comfortable with it. However, each time she does tell the truth and is recognized for it, she is one step closer to earning everyone's trust. Her father told her teacher about the come back, who began to implement it within her classroom. She offered the opportunity for anyone to come back about anything and said that many children self-reported mistakes they had made. She said the dynamics of her classroom had changed for the better with less tattling and more children telling the truth.

### Natural Consequences

It is important for children to be responsible for the things they lie about, and a natural consequence needs to be determined. For instance, when asking a child if he ate the three cookies on a plate and he responds with a lie but then comes back to tell the truth, the immediate parental response should be verbal praise for telling the truth. The next step should be to ask him what he thinks should happen as a result of lying about eating those three cookies. If he cannot come up with an answer, then you might suggest that he not have cookies in his lunchbox tomorrow or he needs to skip dessert tonight. Empower your child, and when appropriate, allow him choose his consequences, which will be more meaningful for him.

## Off to the Grocery Store!

Shopping can be complete madness with a young child if you're not prepared. Stress levels of both children and parents seem to rise in stores. I see lots of crying children out and about. Many have learned that, if they cry loud enough or long enough, they will get what they want, such as a toy or some candy to quiet them. Parents handle their crying children in different ways. Some parents yell or threaten, while some give in out of embarrassment and buy the candy. Some parents may refuse to take their child to the store and put off shopping until they can shop alone. That gives a child tremendous power. It also minimizes exposure to and exploration of the world around him. It is easy to set your child up for success and provide experiences to increase interest, good behavior, and self-esteem.

Design a shopping board with your child to create interest and the ability to easily include him in your weekly purchases. The following process will line out the steps:

- Gather materials, including a small piece of cardboard, a roll of clear contact paper, glue, and tape. Divide the cardboard into food categories, including dairy, meat, fruits and veggies, grains, and other (shampoo, paper towels, and so forth).

- Collect multiple food flyers, and cut out pictures of all the various foods you commonly purchase.

- Choose one item to represent each category across the top of the cardboard to help your child visually identify each category. Help your child glue that picture under the category name. For example, glue a picture of milk under the dairy category and hamburgers under the meat category.

- For long-lasting protection, place clear contact paper over the board as well as on all of the pictures of foods you have collected from various flyers. Trim and sort the pictures with your child into the five groups. Store each group (dairy, meat, and so forth) in its own plastic zip bag, and place the five small bags into one large plastic zip storage bag. Connect the large plastic bag and the cardboard with a hole punch to keep the pictures with the board.

- As you make your marketing list during the week, help your child tape the pictures of the items you need on his shopping board. Make him aware of the things that are on the board and the things that are not on the board (candy, cookies, and such). At the store, have him identify the items you need, place them in the cart, remove the pictures from his board, and place them back in a plastic zip bag.

If you have more than one child, you can engage them by assigning jobs. Provide them with job titles and assignments, such as a board holder, a shopper, and the picture keeper, who places the pictures back into the plastic bags.

For a less involved shopping board, purchase a small dry erase board to engage your child at the store. Before you leave, draw simple pictures (loaf of bread, milk, ice cream cone, and so forth) to provide visuals of the things you need. Your child can wipe off or check mark the items that have been placed in the cart. Another alternative is to use a clipboard and draw simple items on paper, providing a colored pencil for your child to color in the items once they have been found.

Engaging your child in these ways will help him feel involved and important, minimizing the chance for undesirable behaviors. Providing lots of praise for great shopping and great listening will help keep your child happy and safe. You can comfortably transition to other types of stores, providing the information and boundaries of what you will be buying and what you will not be shopping for. Do not feel the need to bribe your child or pick up a little something each time you go to the store. Parents who buy their child something each time they go out teach the child to expect something each time they shop. Remember, if you give in at the checkout, you are teaching your child to cry for what he wants until he gets it. When shopping, set your mobile phone alarm, and provide praise every ten minutes for keeping up, helping out, and being the best little shopper ever. That is much better than rewarding with candy. For examples and pictures of how to create your own shopping boards, visit www.yourperfectchild.com and click the "Make Your Own" tab.

## Teaching Table Manners

Many children have a difficult time in a restaurant. They are easily bored and become loud, so parents provide bread and soft drinks to quiet them. By the time their meal arrives, they are completely full, bored, and loud again. Teaching restaurant manners at home can be easy and fun as it prepares them for those special times when you do go out for a family meal. Children can learn restaurant manners as a game, as they remember to chew with their mouth closed, use a napkin, and keep their hands in their lap. Start your own family restaurant in your home to teach the skills you want to increase.

To incorporate manners in your family restaurant, design a file folder to stand on the table. Print your family restaurant name across the top. Under your family restaurant name, write "Restaurant Rules," and list four simple rules:

- **Rule 1:** Chew with your mouth closed. (Draw lips.)

- **Rule 2:** Place napkin in your lap, and wipe your mouth. (Glue on a paper napkin.)

- **Rule 3:** Place hands in lap, and keep elbows off the table. (Draw a hand.)

- **Rule 4:** Speak quietly (almost a whisper) at the table, and do not talk loudly. (Draw an ear.)

Use the opposite side of the file folder to draw "Ordering Rules" that you feel are important. Draw a loaf of bread with one slice, which indicates he may have one piece of bread at the table. Draw one glass, indicating he may have one drink, so as not to fill up before the food arrives. Determine what other rules you feel will help him be successful at the table, and identify those rules with simple drawings that are easily identified.

Review all the restaurant rule pictures with your child and ask him to identify each when you call out the number. If he talks with his mouth full of food during dinner, simply provide a visual, and hold up one finger so he can refer to the rule chart. If he needs to use his napkin, hold up two fingers. Tell him that, when he can identify all the rules by number, you will celebrate at a restaurant to show off his manners!

There are many job opportunities in a restaurant, so offer those to your children as you prepare and serve each meal. Your child can be an assistant chef, the table setter, the wait staff/server, or the busboy who clears the table. Rotate jobs, and allow your child to experience all of them. Be sure to emphasize manners, using "please" and "thank you" so your child will be ready to order.

For complete restaurant success, fill a canvas bag with dot-to-dot books, bubbles, colored pencils, a dry erase board, and so forth. Keep this bag only for use at a restaurant, not at any other time. It will help to keep him engaged and quiet while everyone is waiting to be served. A SuccessBag™ was developed for restaurants and other outings and can be viewed or purchased at www.yourperfectchild.com.

Nagging or providing repetitive directives may remediate an immediate problem, but it will not instill long-term manners. Teach your child with a game, with the incentive of celebrating at a restaurant, so he will learn to take pride in his new skills. While dining at the restaurant, identify the job that people are doing. Encourage your child to use his ordering manners, as you practiced at home. You will be delighted when other customers stop by your table to compliment your child's delightful behavior and wonderful manners.

## Use a Puzzle to Improve Behavior

Recognize your child's many positive behaviors throughout each day to help him develop self-confidence. When a child feels confident, he has less need to act out for negative attention. This will affect his overall social functioning and academic performance. Some parents do not feel they should have to teach their child what to do, believing that kids should know how to behave because they have been told several times. Children learn by watching, doing, and listening. They try what they see, and they repeat what they hear. Children learn through appropriate modeling, opportunity for exposure, and recognition of their successes. Some parents also feel that, once they have told their child what is expected, there is no need to recognize or praise that accomplishment. However, children learn quickly when they are continually recognized or praised for what they have done well.

The type of attention you provide will determine your child's success. There are many different approaches or parenting styles. Some of which will actually ignite negative, attention-seeking behavior. Watch what you say and how you say it. Some parents might argue, "I'm not the problem here, so why should I have to change what I'm doing? Why do I need to give him a pat on the back for every little thing he does well?" Simply put, although you may not be the problem, you can be the solution. Your child cannot change his behavior without your help. So jump in, and commit to improving your child's behavior by recognizing the positive things he does throughout each day. Recognize efforts with verbal praise, physical touch, and a tangible incentive.

## Create Puzzle Pieces for Great Behavior

Define great behavior with your child. Ask if fighting with his brother will earn him a puzzle piece. Ask if sharing will earn him a puzzle piece. Explain that sharing, kindness, and listening the first time will earn a puzzle piece.

- Save the front flap of your child's favorite cereal box. On the reverse of the front, draw simple puzzle shapes and number each piece, up to ten. Cut and place those pieces in an envelope. The puzzle pieces are the tangible incentive you can give to your child for really great behavior.

- Place the envelope of puzzle pieces in a small basket or box. As your child listens the first time, shares nicely, or puts away a toy without a reminder, provide verbal recognition, a gentle touch to provide sensory communication, and a puzzle piece.

- As you recognize great behavior throughout the day, provide puzzle pieces, and help your child tape the pieces together. Your child will become excited with the puzzle as well as improve his behavior because he has your recognition and attention. Do not use the pieces for bribery. Bribery does not teach self-control or self-regulation.

- Choose a grand prize when the puzzle is complete. An intrinsic reward might be to make ice cream sundaes together, go for a hike, or play a board game of his choice. Those rewards are lasting and meaningful rather than an extrinsic reward, such as a toy.

When you give a puzzle piece, describe the action that earned it. Saying "good boy" is not enough to improve a behavior. Tell your child exactly what you are pleased about, saying, "I'm glad you threw out your paper plate." This is recognition directly related to the behavior you want to continue. If you feel you should not need to praise a behavior but understand the importance of recognition, give a factual narrative, "I see you threw your paper plate in the trash." That tells your child that you are watching what he is doing and recognizing his efforts. Do not ever threaten or take puzzle pieces away for bad behavior. Your child earned those pieces for specific behaviors, which you want to continue. When you focus on the positives, you will be amazed by how happy and well behaved your child can be.

# Dear Diana

*I'm on the Phone!*

Dear Diana, I have a two-year-old daughter. I run a small business from my home, and whenever I get on the phone to make appointments, my daughter inevitably needs my attention or cries out. Needless to say, it is very disruptive for my work, and she isn't happy either! Do you have any suggestions for how I can teach her to be quiet and to wait while I make my calls? Phone Mom

⁓

Dear Phone Mom, Yes, you can absolutely teach your child to be patient and quiet while you are on the phone by training her in small, incremental steps over the course of several days. Most times, a child will interrupt while we are on the phone, simply looking for attention. Set your child up for success with this three-step training process, eliminating your need to do, answer, get, or fix something. The first step is the most detailed and the most important.

- **Teach.** Bend down, touch your child, and say you are going to make an important call. Tell her you want to be very sure she has everything she needs while you are talking. Choose a drink, a small snack, and a fun activity that she can do independently (coloring, building blocks, and a book). Set everything up in one area, and ask if there is anything else she needs before you make your call. Teach her a secret reminder code, and tell her that it is very important for her to be very quiet while you are on the phone. Say, "If you forget, I'll give you the secret reminder code. I will always come to get you as soon as I am off the phone, and I will be so proud of you for being so quiet." Teach simple, effective codes, including "Shhhh" with one finger on the lips. She may love to see you puff your cheeks, as if blowing up a balloon, and refering to it as "catch a bubble." When you do the catch a bubble code, she will remember to catch a bubble herself and wait patiently. You might display a "stop" gesture with your hand, showing one or five fingers to indicate how many minutes you will be on the phone.

- **Test.** The second step is to make a brief call within eyesight and earshot of your child. Call anyone or no one, but be certain that the conversation is under two minutes so your child is still engaged in her activity and successful by remaining quiet.

- **Praise.** Finally, when you hang up from your call, get up and go to your child. Make a gentle connective touch, and give a verbal praise, stating how proud you are that she "was so quiet" while you were on the phone. Spend a few extra minutes with your child, as your attention is her reward for patience and her quiet behavior.

Follow these three steps several times a day every day for about a week. Each day, you can lengthen each subsequent call by one minute longer. If you are consistent, your child should become well trained, enabling you to make your business calls. Many families who have implemented this pattern have become interruption-free. Most importantly, remember that your daughter needs your attention, so keep your phone calls as short as possible and lavish praise for her patience.

# 5

# Temper Tantrums

## Introduction: Nobody Likes a Temper Tantrum!

Approximately 70 percent of toddlers have a least one temper tantrum per day.[26] Temper tantrums are tough to endure. They evoke a wide range of feelings in parents, sometimes making them feel incapable, inadequate, or even incompetent in their position as a parent. Those feelings usually evolve into embarrassment, frustration, and then anger, leading some parents to feel they do not have control and are therefore out of control. A child who senses that his parent is not in control can become unsettled and display attention-seeking behavior. Common questions that parents ask include: Why can't he just do what I ask? Why does he have to be so headstrong? Why is parenting so tough? Why doesn't anyone else seem have this problem with him? What am I doing wrong, and why does he love to push my buttons? A variety of clearly defined interventions described in this chapter can diminish tantrums and aggressive behaviors.

## Why Do Children Tantrum?

Children melt down, tantrum, act out, or become aggressive for a variety of reasons. Young toddlers can become easily frustrated when they can't communicate their wants or needs due to immature language skills. They are told "no" and have things taken away from them, either for safety or disciplinary reasons, throughout the day. Their frustration can lead to aggressive behavior, including biting, hitting, kicking, and hair pulling, to

---

26  *The Incredible Years*, 17.

name a few. Children also fall victim of the acronym HALT, which stands for hungry, angry, lonely, and tired. When one or more of those describes your child, you can be certain that he is going to melt down.

Another precursor to meltdowns is the manner in which you present a directive. How you communicate your expectations will often determine the outcome of how your child responds or complies. When you get a no from your child, do you escalate out of anger from zero to ten, or do you take a breath, connect with your child, and calmly repeat your expectation? Some children have a temper tantrum because they have learned that a great deal of attention is provided when they scream. You might say that these children have been trained to tantrum, as their unruly behavior motivates their parents to give in and give him what he wants just so he will stop screaming. Most parents will say they give their child constant attention, so he should not need to seek negative attention with a tantrum. However, the type of attention you give to your child will directly impact the behavioral outcome. Simple steps to redirect and remediate behaviors are found in this chapter, with an emphasis on providing positive strategies to meet the needs of the moment.

## Changing Behaviors

To be most successful in changing your child's behavior, you will need to change your automatic responses, your wiring, or your entire electrical panel so old buttons don't work anymore for your child. You need to pull things apart and really take the time to think about the problem at a time other than when the problem is occurring.[27] When you focus on the "wh" questions (why does this happen, when does this happen, where does this happen, and with whom does this happen), you can approach the problem in a constructive way, develop a thoughtful parenting plan, and make a conscious effort to consistently follow through every time with the same response.

Think of all the ways you have tried to change your child's behavior. Have you yelled, threatened, given time-outs, and then given up? The expression "nothing changes if nothing changes" comes to mind. When you change your mind-set and decide to teach and retrain your child with new ways to behave, you will be amazed with your success. Remember that consistency is instrumental in retraining your child. Did you ever notice that some parents seem to have children who are quiet and respectful

---

27  *Developmental Profiles: Pre-Birth through Eight*, 82.

and follow directions? A teaching approach and parenting style molds, guides, and shapes a child. Watch that parent to learn how he handles misbehaviors, noncompliance, tantrums, or rude behaviors, as well as how he pays attention to all the small wonderful things his child does. That is the key to changing behaviors. When your child does what he is told, shares with another, picks up after himself, makes an attempt, or is thoughtful, rigorously focus on that behavior, providing continuous recognition. You will soon see improved behavior, compliancy, and confidence. It is not magic; it is human nature. We all want to be recognized for the nice things we do or the achievements we make. As a parent, you may forget, get too busy, or just expect our child to do as he is told. However, a deed unrecognized is a deed in jeopardy. Children learn from their successes and build upon them. It is critical to provide extensive positive recognition for the behaviors you want to continue. Read more about providing appropriate recognition in the Communication chapter.

## Defusing and Distracting

There are many ways in which to deter a child as he is escalating, but it is nearly impossible to defuse a full-blown tantrum. Watch closely and develop awareness as your child starts to escalate from zero to ten. When he is at levels one, two, or three, you can often redirect or distract with success. A child in a full-blown, out-of-control tantrum is not able to pull himself together simply because you are telling him to do so. He will need to learn how to de-escalate on his own. A successful method of teaching self-regulation is to walk away and provide a safe, quiet space with no audience and no fuel for his fire. I have prompted many parents to remove themselves from a spiraling, out-of-control tantrum when they have typically responded with coaching, prompting, demanding, begging, or bribing with a negative result. Unfortunately, sometimes when a parent changes their behavior and walks away, the child will escalate (throw or break something), attempting to get his parent to respond as he did in the past. That is called an extension burst.[28] This can be eliminated with consistency. Read more in this chapter to learn, step by step, how to minimize or eliminate tantrums and aggressive behavior. Understand and believe that you can change any behavior with a behavior plan, compassion, and consistency.

---

28  *How to Behave So Your Child Will, Too*, 109.

# Misbehaving or Misunderstood?

Many things can add to morning stress, one of which may be a child who refuses to get dressed. I have worked with so many families whose child is completely intolerant of the feeling of an uneven sock seam, the rough feeling of jeans, the sandpaper feeling of a shirt, or even the seams of a tag at the collar. A child may not necessarily be able to express his discomfort, so his behavior may present with screaming or refusal to dress. Dressing a child for school can be challenging enough, but dressing a child who cannot tolerate the feeling of socks or shoes can send you over the edge.

Many parents are unaware of potential sensory issues that can significantly affect a child's behavior. One of my sons, now very successful and working on Wall Street, had to have his sock seam exactly straight across the toe line every morning, no matter how late we were running. If it were not perfect, his shoes came off, and we had to reseam until he was comfortable. I learned to turn his socks inside out, keeping the seam away from his skin. He had acute hearing, so I removed his bedroom clock because the ticking kept him awake. And, believe it or not, he could smell vanilla ice cream from another room. Heightened sensitivities can become a disability because a child remains focused on the sensation and is unable to attend to other learning. However, I know firsthand that success is limitless if a parent becomes educated and dedicated to work with what could otherwise be thought to be a defiant, difficult child.[29]

A mom contacted me in tears, saying her son was ruining their household. He refused to dress for school, fighting and screaming as she put on his clothes every single day. We talked about the items he was comfortable wearing, which were a total of three pairs of pants and five shirts out of his entire closet. I suggested books for her to read to learn about sensory processing disorder and provided a lot of information for her to digest. I suggested she only purchase clothing that he had tried on and he should wear them around the house to see if he remained comfortable before the tags came off. We developed the plan that, after his bath each night, he would get dressed in his next day's school clothes to be sure those clothes were comfortable. Just before bed, he changed into his pajamas, and his school clothes were laid out for the next morning. Any morning difficulty could then be identified as behavioral since the clothes were worn comfortably the previous evening. That was more than a year ago, and today, Joey has expanded his tolerance as well as his wardrobe. Contact

---

29  *Raising Your Spirited Child*, 115.

your pediatrician and discuss an occupational therapy evaluation if you feel your child may have sensory processing difficulties.

Another area of concern that can directly affect behavior is allergies. I have worked with many children who have had severe reactions to food, soaps, or medications, and their reactions manifested into aggressive behaviors. Review the use of new detergents, allergy medications, quantities, or varieties of chemicals or dyes in processed food as an important first step in determining the cause of misbehaviors. Review your family history for illness and allergies to eliminate uncertainty and find your answers.

Years ago, I worked with the parents of a three-year-old with koumpounophobia, a fear of buttons. She violently refused to wear anything with buttons and screamed if her mom approached with buttons on her shirt. Many thought she was totally noncompliant and needed to be forced or punished, but that did not resolve the issue. Mom learned to accept that the pretty clothes with buttons were not going to be worn, and if she wanted to hold her daughter, she needed to remove her own buttons. The little girl gradually learned to sit near others with buttons and developed self-regulating techniques of hand washing when she came in direct contact with a button. Although your child may not have koumpounophobia, it is important to be aware, to acknowledge, and to accept that your child may be exhibiting misbehaviors due to an underlying cause. Children cry out for help in a variety of ways. We need to listen, watch closely, and love them, no matter what. Over time, tolerance and healing can occur with therapeutic exposure, effort, and support from family and professionals.

## Take Five Minutes to Change Your Child's Behavior

It is absolutely amazing how five or ten minutes of your time can improve your child's behavior. When parents get home from work, they may just want to change out of work clothes and decompress. Coincidentally, that is often the time your child will escalate his attention-seeking behaviors. Some parents might be familiar with the term "the 5:00 witching hour" or "the mother hour," as my mom used to call it. Those phrases refer to when kids are hungry, tired, and wanting or needing help or attention. Providing your child with a few minutes of positive, focused attention could eliminate hours of evening stress.

I worked with a family whose little boy became destructive the moment his dad came home from work. He tore through the house, chased after the dog, and knocked things over, demanding that Dad look at his building blocks or coloring work. His dad just wanted a few minutes alone to take off his coat, catch his breath, and go through the mail. His son learned how to get his attention with yelling and spankings. They were in a destructive cycle. I asked questions to determine the motivating factors for this little boy to misbehave. I asked about his overall behavior, how much time he spent with his dad in the evenings or on weekends, and what routines were in place. The parents reported that their son was generally happy, could follow routines, and could engage with other children appropriately. He "just went crazy" around dinnertime when his dad came home.

I suggested that his mom offer a very small, nutritious snack around 4:00 to eliminate his hunger. I asked his dad if he would consider spending five or ten minutes with his son as soon as he came in the door rather than taking time alone or checking the mail. I prompted their son to choose a book or game that his dad could enjoy with him when he got home. I suggested that his dad call when he was close to home, so his son could be ready and waiting on the couch with his book or game. Everyone was set up for success. As a result, their son felt important, more important than the mail. He quickly learned to self-regulate his attention-seeking behaviors, knowing he had his dad's full attention for the first few minutes each night. The destruction, yelling, and spankings stopped. Dad created an opportunity to build a positive relationship with his son, and their evenings became calm and enjoyable.

Another story comes from my own experience of raising my two boys, who are twenty months apart in age. I continually fostered successful playtimes to increase their sibling relationship because I wanted them to be the best of friends. By the time they reached three and four years old, they had learned to share and play nicely with many of the same interests. Each day, I set them up in their playroom with dinosaurs, plastic mountains, and a desert mural that my dad painted. Usually there were disagreements, including who had which dinosaur or how they should build the jungle with their blocks. Inevitably, there was tattling and whining. I found it discouraging that my boys were not successful in playing for longer periods of time and frustrating to know that I had to referee a disagreement every twenty minutes. Telling them to play nicely did not change their behavior. Yelling certainly did not encourage them to play together, and separating them was exactly the opposite of what I was trying to foster, to teach them to play together.

I realized I was responding to their inability for extended play rather than teach the skills they needed to negotiate and accommodate each other. Teaching requires time, so I set a timer every fifteen minutes, just before a breakdown might have occurred. I sat with them and praised their play and their sharing for a full five minutes before returning to my chores. After several positive interventions, I increased my timer to twenty, twenty-five, and then thirty minutes. The boys were happy to show me what they had built and learned to play cooperatively, sometimes for hours. I learned firsthand that five little minutes, filled with positive attention, can dramatically improve a child's behavior.

## HALT! Watch for These Signs to Minimize Meltdowns

Hungry, angry, lonely, and tired (HALT) identifies behavioral triggers. HALT has applied to each of us at one time or another. It definitely applies to children because they are less mature, less patient, and less tolerant of the things that are out of their control. If a parent becomes aware of these triggers, watching his child closely, he can avoid potential meltdowns and temper tantrums in many situations.

- **Hungry.** When we are hungry, we are distracted and irritable. So when you are heading out on errands or appointments, be sure your child has eaten something to carry him over to the next meal. Keep a fully stocked ready-to-go bag in the refrigerator with healthy favorites such as cheese sticks, granola bars, crackers, cut apples, or raisins. It will ensure that your child will not have a meltdown due to hunger.

- **Angry.** When we are angry or upset, we are more likely to be on edge or perhaps snap at someone without cause. When your child is upset, recognize it, and give empathy to defuse a potential meltdown. If your child feels heard or understood, he is less likely to display explosive behaviors. Bend down to your child's level, touch him gently, and speak in a quiet voice. Tell him that you can see he is upset. Distract him by offering a glass of water, a rock in the rocking chair, or a walk outside. These loving, attentive gestures may provide the attention your child needs in order to learn how to self-regulate or de-escalate.

- **Lonely.** For children, lonely equals boredom, which leads to attention-seeking behaviors. Schedule a specific time to spend with your child each day so he can count on your full attention. Stick a note with a picture prompt on the refrigerator to show your chosen activity for the day, such as a favorite book or board game, a swing set, or a bike. Make a commitment to your child that you will spend that special time with him each day. Misbehaviors will diminish when he knows he will have your full attention with a fun activity.

- **Tired.** This one is simple. We are all cranky and irritable when we have not had enough rest, so be realistic with your expectations. Do not take your child out around naptime, and do not take him out if he has not slept well the night before. Keeping children up late at night, skipping naps, or haphazard bedtime schedules will set your child up for failure. A well-rested child is able to explore and enjoy the day with more self-control than a child who is tired.

## Defuse Tantrums with Empathy

The word "empathy" means to show care, concern, or understanding. Offering your child empathy is a very powerful approach to defusing potential meltdowns. We would all do well with a little empathy when we are upset. Our moods stabilize faster when others are empathetic toward us. Empathy sends the message that someone cares.

When a child asks, begs, or whines for a cookie, a parent's first response might be to say, "No, you can't have cookies. It's almost dinnertime. You know that!" Negativity and criticism strip self-confidence and self-esteem. However, when you provide empathy, you have an opportunity to minimize or avoid a meltdown as well as teach your child basic coping skills and patience.

Change your answer from no to yes, because as soon as a child hears "no," he stops listening to the rest of your answer. Respond with, "Yes, you may have a cookie right after dinner. We can choose it right now and wrap it up to keep it fresh." Answering yes and then distracting or redirecting your child by taking out and wrapping the cookies may settle him into acceptance, eliminating a meltdown. Initially, he may start to cry to see if you will change your mind. However, if you consistently respond in the same manner, he will learn to accept your answer. If he does escalate, remind him that he may have a cookie and, whenever he is ready, he may wrap it up for after dinner. Encouraging your child to choose and wrap his cookie is a distraction from escalating emotions. It shows him that you care how he feels, with the satisfaction of having the cookie he wants after dinner. The boundary is set, and the tantrum will have been defused. This may take practice for both of you, but the principle of showing that you care while maintaining the rules (no cookies before dinner) is extremely effective.

Children hear the word "no" all day long. Naturally, it is very frustrating and tantrum provoking to be told "no" repeatedly. Parents cannot and should not say "yes" just to avoid confrontation. They can respond differently, providing empathy with indifference, which means being thoughtful but consistent with your rules. Your child will learn to communicate better and accept boundaries while minimizing impulsivity. Think about how different your day could be with a little empathy.

## Set Your Child Up for Success!

Are you heading to a family gathering or planning to travel on a long-distance trip? Are you going to a restaurant or heading to a doctor appointment? Wherever you are planning to take your young child, be sure to set him up for success by packing a special bag of his own, filled with new, interesting, engaging items to hold his attention. Anticipation, anxiety, uncertainty, boredom, impatience, or overstimulation can all lead to acting out, attention-seeking behaviors. One way to avoid meltdowns and misbehaviors is to provide your child with a sturdy canvas bag filled with interesting items. These items should be age appropriate so they can be used independently when you are not available to entertain, distract, or redirect. I created just such a bag for my son, who was twenty months old when he transitioned from being an only child to the big brother. Although I wanted to give him my complete attention, that was unrealistic with a new baby. I constantly looked for ways to provide him with stimulating, educational experiences yet keep him safe while I was caring for his new baby brother. I knew the toy bin did not always hold interest for him, and many of those toys required my assistance or attention. I did not feel that sticking him in front of the TV was an option. So I gathered items that he could manipulate independently. I taught him that these items were only to be brought out when I was taking care of his brother.

I designed a special canvas bag with feeling faces (happy, sad, scared, and tired) on the front of the bag, so he could learn to identify emotions as a quiet activity. I filled his bag with a windup train, some pop-up books, a large chunky puzzle, a small bottle of bubbles, and his favorite soft toy, Lester. His bag was kept on the floor of the front hall coat closet, so he could access it with independence when he was allowed to use it. He learned the rules and knew he was only permitted to play with those items during specific times in order to keep the newness and excitement. That was the key. His special bag provided him with an opportunity to explore, learn, and remain engaged while I cared for his baby brother. This special bag kept him interested and safely occupied so we took it to restaurants on plane or car trips or while we were waiting for long appointments or visiting relatives. We named it his SuccessBag™ because he played so successfully for such long periods of time. My pediatrician remarked that he wished all patients brought a SuccessBag™ to his waiting room. Friends requested an age-appropriate SuccessBag™ for their children because they work! Over time, I introduced new items. A pack of cards became letter or number identification flash cards or a sorting game, and a small pocket flashlight provided endless fascination. I always had a well-stocked diaper bag, plenty of food, and a SuccessBag™ at the ready.

Since that time, I've worked with hundreds of families who have used a SuccessBag™ for travel, long waiting room stays, appointments, restaurants, and more. They have found that it is easier and much more pleasant to set up their child for success rather than to yell and distract or constantly entertain and redirect. I worked with a family who had sewn their two children's bags out of fabric from their grandma's old dress, so the children could take memories of their grandma with them everywhere they went. Popular smartphones offer apps with games and videos, but those can become tiresome to little ones who learn well with age-appropriate manipulatives that they can twist, turn, jiggle, or blow. Strengthen imagination and creativity as your child interacts and learns from the special items stored in his own SuccessBag™. Read more or purchase your personalized SuccessBag™ at www.yourperfectchild.com.

As my family expanded to three children, there were countless family gatherings, endless appointments, and ongoing obligations. I found that, when each child had his own bag, each remained happy, interested, engaged, quiet, and appropriate. As each child grew up, I continuously increased the skill, interest, and independence level of the items included within each bag. No matter what your child's age, you can minimize meltdowns and public exhibitions while setting your child up for success by providing interesting, creative, educational, exciting materials. You can call it an Out-and-About Bag, an On-the-Go Bag, or even a SuccessBag™. It really doesn't matter what you call it. Just bring the bag!

# Identifying Behaviors

There are many reasons why children display aggressive behaviors, but it is rarely out of a desire to hurt another person. Sometimes, aggression builds from complete frustration or a child's inability to communicate. Sometimes, what a child sees his parent model at home causes aggressive behavior. Sometimes, aggression develops from of retaliation or anger, and sometimes, a child becomes aggressive simply because he is bored. It does not matter because, simply put, aggression is unacceptable. There is a difference between aggressive behavior and annoying, attention-seeking behavior. Different behaviors require different interventions.

## *Annoying Behavior*

A child looking for attention often displays annoying behaviors. You can decrease these behaviors when you:

- Compliment your child on something he did well
- Pay more attention to all positive behaviors so negative behaviors will decrease
- Redirect or distract your child with something of interest to him
- Watch for signs of boredom or other triggers, such as hunger or being tired
- Let your child know that you are not going to give in, whether or not he has a temper tantrum
- Show a stop sign with your hand up, and then walk away

You can choose your battles. It is not necessary to engage with your child each and every time he decides to whine, beg, or misbehave for your attention. You can use the strategies listed previously. Remember to stop … and walk.

## *Learned Behavior*

Toddlers often pull hair, bite, or even hit while being held. I have seen some parents biting their child back or pulling their hair to teach their child how it feels. I have seen others hit their child while yelling, "Don't hit!" Those behaviors are ineffective because they are mixed messages. Children need a clear understanding in order to learn what is expected of them. Learn to speak slowly in a low tone of voice, saying, "No pulling hair," while placing your child down on the ground. That will teach your child that he will not be held when he pulls hair. Be consistent, and follow through with the same response each time. This will ensure that, after several experiences of being placed down, he will not hit or pull hair if he wants to be held. Many families have eliminated unwanted behaviors by following that same, simple procedure. I have attended multiple events where show dogs or other animals have been successfully trained, sometimes with only hand signals. Your child is definitely more capable than a show animal, so be confident, teach with patience, and train with love and consistency.

## Physically Aggressive Behavior

Taking it to the next level; that is, when a child displays deliberate, aggressive behaviors that involve another child, an adult, or even an animal, immediately and firmly address the exact misbehavior, and then go to the target. Assisting the target takes the attention away from the aggressor. For those parents who feel that spanking or yelling is the only way to stop aggressive behavior, take time to evaluate whether spanking or yelling does eliminate that behavior. Does your child, who is yelled at or spanked, continue to hit, bite, kick, or scratch? If so, then the spanking is not working. A replacement behavior needs to be taught, and your child needs to receive more positive attention than negative. Sadly, through the eyes of a child, negative attention is better than no attention at all. A child will misbehave if he feels that it is the only way to get attention. Remember "What's In It For Me" or WIIFM. If a child is successful in receiving attention for a behavior, that behavior will increase with a response or an audience.

Nothing changes if nothing changes. This means that, if your current response or discipline is not changing or improving your child's behavior, then perhaps it is time to try something new. I read that the definition of insanity is when we keep doing the same thing over and over but expect a different result. Are you yelling and spanking to stop your child from aggressive behaviors, but your child continues to hit? Maybe it is time to think about a change.

Much of my work has been with families who their preschool has referred because their child was aggressive or at risk of being expelled at two, three, or four years of age. The parent was given a choice: either learn new strategies to eliminate their child's hitting or biting or find a new preschool. I had the opportunity to model a successful three-step intervention for a mom and dad when their four-year-old son deeply scratched his five-year-old sibling for no apparent reason. If you ask a child, "Why did you do that?" he will say, "I don't know." Or he might say, "He was bothering me." So don't ask. Children display aggressive behaviors because they get something out of it, usually lots of attention. We yell, spank, and send them to time-out, where they get up, only to be placed back down. An alternative three-step process works when it is done with consistency because it identifies the unacceptable behavior and provides appropriate attention to the target, not on the aggressor.

1. Do not yell from across the room. Instead, immediately get up and go to the aggressor. Firmly hold the area he used (chin for a biter, hand for a hair puller or hitter, or foot for a kicker). In a deep voice, say very slowly, "You may not (bite, kick, or hit)." Do not say, "We don't bite!" because "we" didn't bite! Keep your attention focused on the aggressor, and watch your language. This is not meant to scare or frighten a child but to clearly identify the unacceptable behavior.

2. Quickly go to the hurt target with lavished attention. "Are you all right? Would you like ice on it? Would you like a glass of juice? I'm so sorry you were hurt." Stay with the target, and as much as possible, give your complete attention. Do not provide eye contact or reengage with the aggressor at this time.

3. When the aggressor approaches, bend down and make a connective touch, quietly saying, "When you are ready to say I'm sorry for (biting, kicking, or pulling hair), then you can be with us. You hurt your (sister, brother, or friend) when you bit (him or her)." Then return your attention to the recipient. This is a teaching opportunity, not a punishment.

Telling a child "You can be with us" or "I'm here for you" provides the necessary security of parental, unconditional love he needs in order to recover and reengage with success. Repeat that process for however long it takes. If he tries to distract you, reengage, or ask for a drink, bend down and quietly repeat, "When you say I'm sorry for biting, then you can join us." As soon as that child takes responsibility and apologizes to his target for the exact behavior, accept his apology and move on. Do not lecture, and do not correct his tone of voice. Verbally recognize that he apologized by saying, "I am happy that you were able to apologize." Make a gentle, connective touch so he understands that he is loved and it is over. Do not say, "Thank you for apologizing," as that communicates a different message.

This incremental process can be completely effective when it is done consistently to teach young children that biting or hitting will not be tolerated. Teaching is the key. We need to teach them so they can learn. In working with so many families, I understand it can be very difficult to implement a new intervention, something that requires thought, consistency, and patience, something very different from the way it has been done in the past. However, it is important to remember that nothing changes if nothing changes.

## Time-out!

Time-out can be a great teaching tool as well as a stress reducer for both a parent and a child. When implemented correctly for the right reason, not overdone, and without anger, a time-out can teach an expected behavior as well as provide the foundational setting for de-escalation. Your child will learn what is expected when you verbally identify unacceptable behavior (hitting) and then remove him to a designated area without speaking, except to say, "You may not hit."

Children act out of impulse and frustration, often due to their inability to communicate properly. They need to be taught how to identify their emotions and use their words. They thrive on attention, whether it is negative or positive, and they will do whatever it takes to get that attention. With consistent parenting, they can learn they will receive endless attention, praise, and recognition for the wonderful things they do throughout the day. When thoughtfully removed and given no attention, a child will learn to change his behavior because his misbehaviors are not receiving the same attention any more.

A time-out is behavioral training that, over time, teaches a child to change his behavior due to the limits that are set and the way in which they are set. It trains a child through calm, consistent repetition. It helps an out-of-control child learn to self-regulate or calm down when consistently and thoughtfully placed in a safe area without anger from his parent.

A time-out should be reserved for egregious behaviors (aggressive, out of control, refusal to comply, and so forth).[30] It becomes completely ineffective when it is used improperly or excessively. A child may become

---

30  *The Big Book of Parenting Solutions*, 118.

angry and retaliatory for being punished and isolated repeatedly instead of being taught how to self-regulate with other teaching methods. A time-out can be effective for children age three or older who have developed some reasoning skills and can conceptualize cause and effect.

The more defined and consistent the area, the more successful a time-out will be for your child as he becomes familiar with the procedure. Removal leaves him without an audience for which to perform as well as a place to gain self-control.

A time-out can be provided on a designated step, chair, or couch. I have purchased black pillows for families to teach take-along time-outs, which can be used in a car or at a grandparent's house. A dark, solid-colored pillow (rather than a flowery, bright one) communicates an unspoken message of severity and seriousness. A child need not ever be humiliated in public, but he can be safely removed to a quiet place with his "TO pillow." A designated "sit and think" chair is an alternative name and space for a time-out, yet it provides limits with an opportunity to de-escalate.

A time-out is sometimes viewed as ineffective by parents who yell at their child throughout the process or grab them forcefully as they replace them again and again to the designated area. I often hear, "It just doesn't work. I can't keep him there. He keeps getting up, and I just can't take it." That's the problem. A time-out will not work if you try it a few times, yell throughout the process, and then give up. That inconsistency communicates to your child that all he needs to do is to scream louder or longer in order to get out of his time-out.

Parents definitely provide ammunition and throw gas on their child's emotional fire when they show how angry they are with eyes rolling, sighing, stomping, or yelling. Those actions communicate that they are out of control and cannot control their child's behavior. There is no doubt that placing a young child in time-out can be challenging and stressful. It takes hours of teaching, patience, and dedication to the process, but it is completely successful when done with love and consistency.

I worked with a mom who initiated a time-out with her four-year-old daughter because she continually punched and hit her six-year-old sister. The mom decided she was ready to learn how to successfully implement a time-out. When her daughter became aggressive, she empowered herself as a parent and implemented her first time-out by sitting her daughter on the couch. She telephoned me, saying she had placed her laughing child back on the couch in a time-out sixty-seven times for more than an hour. She was frustrated and near tears. I explained that this time-out was a new consequence for her daughter, who was testing her by laughing and getting off the couch. I encouraged her to be strong, remain consistent, and remember she was teaching her daughter. We reviewed how she should continue to replace her daughter on the couch without emotion or words. Conversation provokes behavior, so she was advised to state, "When you are quiet for four minutes, then you may get up and apologize for hitting." The purpose of a time-out is to teach. Remain calm, and repeat the same words over and over to provide the scaffolding your child needs to learn and self-regulate.

I received a second call after that mom had replaced her child to the couch one hundred and two times. The child was no longer laughing. Instead, she was crying and screaming that she had wet herself. I explained that wetting herself was an attention-seeking behavior. I suggested she ignore the wetting and focus on her child's emotions. I suggested she hold her child briefly for emotional centering and then repeat that one powerful sentence: "When you are quiet for four minutes and ready to apologize, then you may get up from the couch." Shortly after we spoke, her daughter screamed an apology and then quietly said she was sorry. She found her sister, gave her a kiss where she hurt her, and apologized to her as well.

From our prior work together, that mom knew her daughter needed to take responsibility for her own negative, attention-seeking behavior of wetting herself, which she had done in the past when she was angry. She handed her daughter wet washcloths, paper towels for the couch, and clean underwear to change herself. That mom has been successful with time-outs, and that little girl has since decided to place herself in a time-out whenever she feels she needs it.

### The Time-Out Process

Parents who are successful with a time-out understand that it is a process that needs to be taught with patience:

1. Prepare your child in advance by showing him his new area for time-out or "sit and think."

2. Test for understanding, review, and praise his understanding.

3. When it happens, identify the behavior in a low, slow voice, "You may not hit."

4. Walk him, without words, to the designated time-out area, and walk away to set a timer.

5. When he gets up, say nothing. Take a breath, replace him to the area without speaking, and reset the timer.

6. Be prepared for a long trial for the first few times you implement a time-out. If you give in or give up, your child will learn how simple it is to end his time-outs by testing your patience.

7. Every ten times you replace your child, quietly repeat, "When you are quiet for (your child's age) minutes, then you may get up and apologize."

8. When your child does finally comply, give a hug, and say, "I accept your apology for (the exact behavior)."

9. Offer to help him clean up or repair anything that was thrown or damaged.

10. When it is over, move on, and look for all the wonderful things your child will do throughout the rest of the day because he will be looking for ways to please you.

## A Time-Out for Everyone

A parent time-out can be beneficial, especially when sending your child to time-out is not appropriate. Parents are better off removing themselves from the event when they feel they are becoming highly frustrated or escalating in anger. Parents who continue to engage when they are angry may respond inappropriately, out of impulse. Responding in anger will never teach the right lesson. Take a moment alone to compose yourself, take a breath, and decide how to best handle the situation. That is much more effective than yelling, hitting, or threatening. It also models for your child that you know how to stay in control by walking away rather than losing control in the moment. That will always pay off.

Some parents have used the phrase, "Mommy needs a time-out." Although it is wonderful when a parent knows she has reached a boiling point and needs a break, that particular phrase should be eliminated. It sends a mixed message to a child, implying that Mommy has misbehaved. Children understand that a time-out is for those who misbehave. Send a clear message. Say, "I am taking a quiet time (to make my decision or think things over)." This models self-control and removal from a heated situation.

For older children in their tweens and teens, a "blackout of goods and services" is extremely effective and serves the same teaching purpose as a time-out. When a child is in a blackout, he may not use any electronics, enjoy any privileges, ask for car rides, be with friends, engage in conversation, or solicit help or answers from you or any other family member. He will learn that he will receive absolutely no attention until he appropriately apologizes, taking full responsibility for his actions. When implemented appropriately, your child will learn to respond immediately once warned that he is headed into a blackout. Provide this information before you need to use it, explaining the exact details of a blackout as well as your expectations for apologies and taking responsibility.

## Eliminating Time-Out

The best way to teach positive behaviors and minimize the need for a time-out is to model what you want your child to do and then recognize it over and over and over again every time he does it! Verbally identify the exact behavior you just observed ("I just love to watch you share with your sister!") and then reach over to make a gentle connective touch. The behavior you pay attention to will continue again and again.

When training a puppy to sit, we provide lots of praise. Even a year later, when given the command to sit and the dog does, we recognize compliance by providing praise with, "Good dog." Parents need to teach and praise their child at least as consistently as they would with a family dog. Making the effort to continually comment on positive behaviors will absolutely minimize the need for time-outs. Your child will behave appropriately and look for your response whenever he is continually recognized for it.

# Dear Diana

## My Son's Tantrums

*Dear Diana,* I thoroughly enjoy your articles and put your advice to use. I have a soon-to-be four-year-old, and although general discipline has worked well the first four years, I'm still having issues with tantrums. They are not all-out, roll-on-the-ground screaming fits, but if he misses a ball during a game, isn't first in a race, or doesn't get the spot in line he thinks should be his, he simply throws himself on the ground and lies there, like a limp doll. Sometimes, a plaintive whine comes out, but mostly he just lies there with his head in his hands, pouting. It was very embarrassing the other day when he behaved this way during a baseball game at a friend's house. How should I deal with this? Thank you, Mom of an almost four-year-old

⌒

_Dear Mom,_ I commend you on your parenting accomplishments of raising a child who does not exhibit flat-out, roll-on-the-floor tantrums! Also, you should know that you are in good company because, at one time or another, every parent has experienced humiliation or embarrassment brought on by their child. However, when teaching your child, it is more important to focus on what might be the best intervention at the time of a tantrum rather than allow your embarrassment to take over. Reacting to embarrassment will always lead you to be ineffective. It is wonderful that you are addressing this now, as this type of behavior will obviously be frowned upon in organized team sports as he grows older. Developmentally, your son is right on track. Late threes and early fours are wild with wonder and filled with emotion as well as frustration. Children of this age have learned cause and effect, but they continue to test surroundings and circumstances, testing for consistency. Start teaching at home. When you remain dedicated and consistent, you will see remarkable changes in his emotional functioning.

- **Teach.** Teach your son to identify his feelings. Children who learn to express themselves develop self-confidence and higher self-esteem and misbehave less because they can communicate. The more familiar, comfortable, and expressive he becomes with his feelings, the less he will need to act upon them.[31] Post a Feelings Faces Board, located at www.yourperfectchild.com, to help him identify and process his feelings.

- **Play.** Play lots of games at your house, at least one per day. Some parents let their children win all the time, either to help them feel successful or to avoid a tantrum, but neither will teach a child how

31  *Thinking Parent, Thinking Child,* 14.

to be a gracious loser. Instead, winning all the time will teach a child that winning is everything. You should try to win without being overly competitive. When you do win, tell him that you loved playing with him, suggest he congratulate you, and share high fives! Explain where high fives originated from. In 1977, when Dusty Baker, a player for the Dodgers, hit a home run, he approached home plate. The on-deck teammate, Glenn Burke, raised his hand high instead of offering a traditional handshake, making history with a high five. When your son wins, congratulate him, highlighting the fun you had playing with him while minimizing his win. Then offer him a high five! The more exposure he has to appropriate behavior for winning and losing, the more comfortable he will become in public and with his peers.

- **Increase his acts of kindness.** Teach your son what it feels like to hold doors for others or to offer them a spot in line. You can start modeling that in a cashier line, when someone behind you has only a few items and you offer for him to go ahead of you. Talk about how good it feels to do for others. Tell him that you can actually feel your heart fill up. When he does something thoughtful or kind for someone, be sure to recognize it with a hug and a verbal recognition of, "I noticed that you …"

- **Provide boundaries.** Set your son up for success. Remind him of the time he sprawled on the ground at your friend's house, and remark how embarrassed he must have felt. Let him know that his friends want to play with him because he is fun, not because he wins. Tell him that he is not fun to be with when he pouts on the field. Suggest that, if he loses or feels frustrated, he should come to you for help and you will be so proud of him for asking for your help. Tell him that, if he chooses to act out his feelings on the field again, you will go to him to see if you can do anything for him there. Then you will join the other moms and kids. When he tests you, enjoy your teaching moment. Approach him with a loving touch, and tell him he looks upset. Tell him you will help him get back into the game whenever he is ready. Then, as you told him you would do, rejoin your group of moms. Do not encourage him with his attention-seeking behavior. Over time, he will learn how good it feels to be a part of the game, win or lose.

# Dear Diana

*Rough Mornings?*

Dear Diana, My seven-year-old son wakes up in a bad mood every day, which seems to set the tone for the entire day. It is very difficult to wake him up, get him out of bed, and get ready for school. Our mornings are stressful because nothing seems to go right for him. He has become negative and pessimistic. We have always allowed him the freedom to express himself, but it seems he has nothing positive to say and he hardly ever smiles. Please help. Thanks, Looking for a Smile

⌒

Dear Looking For a Smile, Mornings are tough for many children as well as adults. Before he goes to bed, initiate a relaxed conversation with your son, letting him know you see him struggle in the morning. Tell him you would like to help and make it easier for him. Ask him how he would like to wake up each day, and include him in the planning process. Would he like his own alarm clock? Would he like you to tickle him awake or rub his back? Would a glass of water or OJ help to get him going? Check for clarity by repeating what he says.

Ask your son what other ideas might be helpful to get him out of bed and out the door in a happier mood each day. Should clothes be chosen the night before? Should he place his backpack by the door before going to bed? The more involved he is in his game plan, the more invested he will be with the entire process. His choices become his decisions, which empower him. After you commit to your part (waking him up with a glass of water), remind him to commit to his part (waking up with a smile). Change is not easy, but simple steps (discussion, choices, decisions, and commitment) will increase communication, which is critical when identifying underlying issues.

I worked with a mom of an eight-year-old in a similar situation. That little girl asked that her mom put on some quiet music and rub her back for a few minutes before she had to get up. It changed her whole day as well as her overall attitude because her mom was spending a few quality minutes with her each morning rather than yelling for her to get out of bed.

If you do not see improvement, you might consider contacting your pediatrician to eliminate the possibility of low-grade depression, allergies, or other medically related issues that could affect his behavior. It is also important to investigate and eliminate potential social or academic difficulties in school. Determine if your son is getting enough sleep. (Ten to twelve hours is recommended for his age.) Flared tempers and argumentative behavior can show inadequate sleep, simply because it is hard to function when we are tired.

Once you have identified that he is getting enough sleep, focus on an attitude adjustment. Do not focus on his negativity. If he is pessimistic, saying he knows he is going to fail a test, acknowledge it with a positive, brief reply, "You are very bright, and I'll be happy to help you study so you'll be prepared." Offering your help is a supportive approach to turning around a bad situation. It will give him a choice. ("I can complain and fail the test or stop complaining and ask for help.") Perhaps he just needs to learn what it feels like to be happy, optimistic, and successful.

I worked with a child who felt it was better to be pessimistic and not expect anything good to happen so she would not be disappointed. She said that, if something good did happen, it was a great surprise. What a sad way to live. For her, it was simply a negative mind-set that we quickly turned around.

No matter what is affecting your son, you can help him find a reason to smile each day, starting first thing in the morning.

# 6

# Setting Limits

## Introduction: Consistency, Limits, and a Lot of Love

Setting limits can be a struggle for many parents. Some find it difficult to enforce their rules with consistency, so they look for excuses to change them. Some think of setting limits as being too strict and worry their child may become angry with them. Some parents simply do not want to be confronted with pushback, negotiation, or the tantrum their child will undoubtedly display when they say, "These are the rules." The good news is that, when you learn how to provide clear, appropriate rules in a relaxed environment, your child will be better able to understand, process, and comply. An inconsistent parent will sometimes enforce the rules and, at other times, not have the strength to follow through. Inconsistency sends an unclear message: "If you push me hard enough or long enough, I'll give in, and you'll get your way."

Children thrive with a consistent routine. It is comforting for them to know with certainty that, each and every time, they know what to expect and what is expected of them. They find comfort in sameness, as displayed when they request the same bedtime story over and over. Changing the rules is stressful and confusing, often causing the exact behavior that parents try to avoid. Some of those behaviors include pushback, negotiation, noncompliance, and meltdowns. It is also important to remember that the world is full of rules, limits, and boundaries, so your child needs to know when enough is enough. He needs to learn how to be compliant and respectful in any situation. It has been said that, when a parent does not teach his child how to live within limits, someone else will, whether it be a school principal or the police.

## Setting Limits

Be kind, and be consistent. Define your expectations, and thoughtfully determine your rules. Present the information simply and clearly at a time other than during the event—that is, when your child is able to process the information. Provide the opportunity for your child to practice the new rule. If your child is old enough to verbalize, ask him to tell you about the new rule. If your child is noncompliant, repeat the rule again in a nonthreatening, even-toned voice. Do not allow your child to locate your electrical circuit box or push your buttons!

Always remain consistent. Provide the same words in the same tone of voice. If you give in, you will teach your child to argue and negotiate. Praise positive behaviors every time to improve behaviors. Read more in this chapter about setting limits and the art of following through. Learn to say what you mean and mean what you say, but don't say it mean. You will feel less frustrated because there will be no reason to yell. Thoughtful, consistent parenting definitely takes practice, but it could be one of the best gifts you ever give to your child. Be an intentional teacher throughout your child's life because loving your child is just not enough.

## Mixed Messages

Children need lots of practice to independently incorporate and actually learn a new skill. It can take a child between thirty and two hundred attempted trials before mastering a skill, depending on the difficulty of the task and the environment. So how can parents best set their children up for success and provide them with the best learning environment? That answer always will be "with consistency."

Children thrive on consistency and predictability. They learn what to expect and what is expected of them. They find comfort in sameness. They request the same story over and over, learning the characters, the story line, and the visual clues until they know it well enough to move on to their next favorite book. They request the same food day after day because there is comfort in knowing the taste and texture. After months of only eating mac and cheese, a parent might buy a few cases (or consider investing in stock), only to find that his child is ready to move on to the next taste test sensation.

Parental inconsistency brings confusion, anxiety, chaos, and an invitation for limit testing. The limit testing wears down a parent, but that is how children learn. They ask, and we answer. They do, and we respond. The consistent answer or response teaches a child to understand how things work so they can accept, incorporate, internalize, and move on. When a parent is inconsistent, a child will try to figure things out through multiple attempts to see if he will get the same response. Children need to test the boundaries to learn the rules. They cry or tantrum out of confusion. Setting limits and being consistent is an effective and positive way to parent. Although very difficult at times, consistency is a true gift.

## A System

You can minimize resistance and tantrums, as well as increase the frequency of desired behaviors, by using the Three Ps:

- **Present the information.** The information is the new skill. Whether it is an abstract or concrete skill, teach it repeatedly with patience. Present the information with consistency and predictability, step by step. Be sure that your expectations are realistic and age appropriate.

- **Provide the opportunity.** Provide continuous opportunity in a variety of environments at different times of the day with various people teaching the skill. Approach it as if you are a teacher, which you are. The more opportunity your child has, the faster he will learn.

- **Praise the behavior.** All efforts should be verbally and physically recognized with a gentle, connective touch. If you think of the training process to teach a puppy to learn to sit, it may be easier to understand how children learn. First, we give the puppy a verbal command, such as "sit." At the same time, we teach what "sit" means by gently pushing down on the puppy's behind. Next, we say, "Good dog for sitting," pat the dog on the head, and give the dog a bone. Presenting consistent information, with multiple opportunities and generous praise for good results, will result in the puppy learning to sit. Why then do we forget to praise our children after they have mastered a skill?

## Quick Tips to Remember

- Do not change the rules, having an expectation one day and then allowing an alternate behavior the next day. That inconsistency will cause confusion and a tantrum.

- Do not reward bad behavior by giving in to a tantrum. Stay cool, and continue to teach your lesson with love.

- Remember that you are your child's most powerful teacher. Parent with purpose, and be an intentional teacher.

## Kids and Car Seats

I recently observed a mom in a parking lot with her young son, who was probably around three years old. I watched as she loaded the car with groceries and repeatedly asked him to climb in the car. "Please get in the car. Dad will be really angry when he finds out that you gave me such a hard time. If you don't get in your car seat, we're not going to the park later." The little boy just sat on the pavement and refused to move. He heard his mother ask when she used the word "please." He heard her turn her parental power over to Dad, who "will be really angry when he finds out." And he heard his mom threaten him with not going to the park. None of it worked, and it rarely does. At one time or another, we have all been in situations where our children test both our patience as well as our parenting skills in public. They sense our discomfort and embarrassment and run wild with it! Some parents will not take control, but they continue to beg, bribe, or threaten their child. They seem to be afraid to physically pick up or move their child, as if they are concerned with what others might think. And that is exactly what their child is hoping for. In this situation, Mom could have taken control in several ways.

- **Take control.** Sometimes, it is necessary to carry your screaming, kicking child and place him where he needs to be. In this case, it is the car seat. Communicate clearly by eliminating requests (please) and using a more controlled, lower tone of voice. Never defer power to someone else, such as the restaurant manager, the police, or another parent. That communicates that you cannot control his behavior. Provide a when and then such as, "When you get in your car seat, then we can head over to the park." Provide an incentive rather than a threat. When carrying a screaming, kicking child, do not address those behaviors at that time. If you become focused on "How dare you kick me!" chances are that he will kick again (and harder) because he got a big response from you. When he can push your buttons, he feels he is taking control of the situation. Carry your child without speaking. Later, when he is calm, show him where he kicked you, and have him touch that spot with his hand, apologizing for his exact behavior. "I'm sorry I kicked you on your leg, Mommy."

- **Remove him to another location.** Sometimes when a child has escalated, there is no going back until he becomes exhausted and de-escalates. That can be the nature of a temper tantrum. When a child learns he will get nothing out of it, he will learn to self-regulate sooner. Forcing an explosive child into a car seat could prove physically dangerous, as well as ineffective, because he might try to fight his way out of it. You will have better success if you remove him from that area, carry him to a quieter, more isolated spot, and hold him without talking. Provide firm down strokes on his head or arm until he de-escalates. Removal from the place where he ignited and an audience usually proves successful within minutes. Rather than pleading, fighting, forcing, or screaming, give him time and a new space.

- **Eliminate empty threats.** Threatening a child, saying you are going to tell Dad or anyone else, is ineffective. It strips you of your parental power every time. You immediately diminish your authority when you tell your child that someone else will handle the situation, indicating you cannot manage his behavior. After a few of those empty threats, your child will become trained to ignore them, and his behavior will escalate as he gains control. Instead of threats, provide incentives in your language, emphasizing when and then. "When you get into your car seat, then we will go home to make your favorite spaghetti dinner."

- **Be consistent.** Your child needs to understand that there are no exceptions to sitting properly in a car seat when it is time to go. A dad asked me if he could just let his son sit in the front seat because it was too much of a struggle to get him into the back. Absolutely not! Safety first! The front of a car is not a safe place for a child. Allowing a child to sit in the front just because it is difficult to get him into a car seat communicates that his strong-willed behavior will get him whatever he wants.

Provide an Out-and-About Bag for car trips, which contains inexpensive, interesting items to engage your child and can be an incentive to get him into his seat. Those items should be safe, fun, and rotated often, which he can use safely and independently while you are driving. That's called setting him up for success!

# Dear Diana

*Setting Clear, Firm Boundaries*

Dear Diana, I have a fifteen-year-old daughter, and we had her fifteen-year-old boyfriend over. Her father caught them making out, with our other daughter (who is ten) in the same room. Her father had me take the boyfriend home immediately and told him to never come back. This has made a very uncomfortable situation here. I don't know how to deal with this because she is my firstborn. I tried to explain to her several times before that boys only want her goodies and nothing else. She has always been very smart and gets good grades in school. I just don't want her to ruin her life. Can you help? Distressed Mom

Dear Distressed, I applaud her father for setting a firm boundary for inappropriate behavior. Some parents find limit setting to be too difficult or uncomfortable to follow through. When you allow something to continue that you do not believe in, you send a message of acceptance for that behavior.

At fifteen, your daughter has a natural interest in boys. Teach her what is acceptable and what you expect of her. Telling her that boys only want her company for one reason tells her she has no value and can't be appreciated for who she is. That may quickly close the door to your communication, leaving her to completely disregard your parental warnings or helpful insight. Rather than use scare tactics to keep her away from boys, focus on helping your daughter to build her self-esteem for all she has accomplished and all you are proud of. She needs to feel good about herself, knowing she is smart, works hard for her grades, and understands she can be liked for many, many reasons. With increased self-esteem, she will learn how to make good decisions for herself, even when you are not there to reinforce or guide her. Teach her your moral values. Talk to her about her future, her hopes, and dreams, with plenty of encouragement to make it all happen. This is how children, tweens, and teens grow up to make important life decisions for themselves. Tell your daughter that you love her too much to allow her to get hurt.

It is very important that her boyfriend was also held accountable for his disrespectful, inappropriate behavior. They both used bad judgment.

Allowing boyfriends or girlfriends in bedrooms sends a mixed message. You have now made your house rules very clear by taking him home and telling him that he is no longer welcome in your home. Trying to keep them apart may be difficult, but you can absolutely prohibit him from coming to your house. Now is a good time to clearly communicate all of your rules and expectations for friendships and dating. Review rules and consequences for curfew, and discuss your rules for visiting with friends when parents are not home. Unsupervised kids get into trouble.

It is unfortunate that your ten-year-old was exposed to her older sister's behavior, as her older sister is a role model. However, your ten-year-old did learn that you will not tolerate inappropriate behavior in your home. You did not mention what she was doing in the room, if her sister told her to keep quiet or if she brought in her father. I do hope that someone took the opportunity to speak thoughtfully with her about what she saw, as ten is a very tender, impressionable age.

Some equate teenage years with volatility. It can be a tough time for everyone. Research done by Dr. Silvia A. Bunge from the University of California at Berkeley states that, although teens may have the cognitive intelligence of an adult, their emotional development lags far behind.[32] Teens seek thrills for new experiences to increase their understanding of life. Those thrills can lead to risky and dangerous behavior. Peers greatly influence teens, and they can become highly self-conscious. They have difficulty delaying gratification and regulating their emotions. Their capacity for reasoning and planning is not fully developed, as their brains are still developing. So although your teen may talk a good game and may sound mature, a lot of brain development needs to occur before healthy, safe decisions can be made. That is why she needs your guidance as her mom.

## Dear Diana

*Teaching Expectations*

Dear Diana, While babysitting our four-year-old grandson, he started spitting, kicking, and throwing things. I explained to him that he wouldn't be allowed to stay with us if his bad behavior continued. I think he has been playing his two parents to the point that they fight at least once a

---

32  www.bungelab.berkeley.edu/conference09/Learning Brain.com

day. We have tried to tell them how damaging their fighting will be on the baby and the whole family. On Friday, after staying with us, we took him home, and when we returned to our home, my husband noticed that our coasters on the table by his chair were missing, as were other things in the house. I called my son-in-law and asked if he could find out what our grandson did with our belongings. When he started to ask, we overheard our daughter intervene and threaten to take the TV out of our grandson's room because he would not tell her. I hung up, telling our son-in-law to just let us know if they found anything. About one hour later, our daughter showed up (after nine at night) with the four-year-old in tow. She was holding his arm, demanding he tell her where all this stuff was. He found each missing item, smiling the whole time. My daughter yelled at me, saying I should have never told him he is not allowed back to our home and she will never let me babysit again. Now with the holidays approaching, what should we do about family gatherings? She hasn't spoken to any of the family. Thank you, Grama

Dear Grama, You have provided a lot of information regarding your family dynamics. It appears that emotions run high and the disconnect is impacting your grandson. You mentioned several things that greatly concern me. I will address four of them:

- You referred to your grandson as "the baby." At four, he is not a baby. To refer to him as a baby sends the message that he is not capable or not responsible for his actions. A four-year-old is an extremely capable child and needs to be recognized for all he can do.

- It concerns me that your grandson has a TV in his room. A television is not a babysitter. It does not replace a parent's role. When story time, quiet, loving whispers, and nighttime kisses replace TV programs, his behavior will improve immediately.

- You mentioned that he is taking items. When items are located, he must return them to the owner, apologize, and take responsibility by doing an act of kindness for that person. Just handing them over does not mean that he understands that he may not take what is not his. Use this type of situation as a learning tool, not a punishment. A full sentence apology ("Grandpa, I'm sorry for taking your coasters,") is a start. He then should ask, "What can I do to show you that I am sorry?" Grandpa could respond, "You can get me a cup of water and place it on my coaster." With that type of teaching, your grandson will have the opportunity to apologize and connect with the items he had taken.

- You said you told him that he would not be allowed to stay with you if his bad behavior continued. Did you speak with him calmly after he de-escalated to identify the unacceptable behaviors of spitting, kicking, and throwing objects?

Your grandson will continue to display misbehaviors until you set firm, consistent boundaries with continuous consequences. He also will continue to display misbehaviors until he is recognized for the positive things that he does well on a regular basis. He needs to learn what that feels like so he will attempt to display more positive behaviors in an attempt to receive more praise. Communicate very clearly, describing exactly what you want.

The adults in your family need to get on the same page. Communication is difficult when no one will break the silence. You might consider calling or sending a note, expressing your love and concern without any blame. Tell your daughter you would like to celebrate the holidays together. If she is unwilling to join family gatherings, then request some special time with your grandson. When he does visit your house, let him know the behaviors you expect. Ask him to repeat back to you his understanding of your expectations. Then give him a big hug.

# Dear Diana

*Respecting House Rules*

Dear Diana, I'm a father of a soon-to-be eighteen-year-old girl. Rules always have been in place and maintained, as she has depended on us for rides. Now that she's mobile, I'm seeking additional language to help communicate my expectations. I'm trying to establish boundaries for when she visits her boyfriend's home. How do I talk to her about not visiting up until curfew just because she has curfew? How do I talk to her about self-respect and appearances? I'm trying to help her manage her reputation. Her curfew is 11:30 p.m. if she is out, but I think that is too late to visit a boy's home. When he comes here, we make sure he leaves by 10:00 p.m. It's an etiquette issue for me. Help? Caring Dad, Marietta, Georgia

～

Dear Caring Dad, I commend you on updating your rules and increasing your communication as circumstances change. There are many things to consider when a new driver becomes licensed, but most importantly, you have a new, inexperienced driver behind a powerful machine, which can end lives in a moment. That requires a respect for driving, parental respect, and respect of house rules.[33] For example, cell phones should be kept in the glove box until the destination is reached, as talking or texting while driving has been equated with driving drunk.

You did not mention who owns the car, who paid for it, or who pays for her car insurance. Those who work toward a financial payment are often more responsible than those who have things given to them. When kids get a license, they tend to disappear. Even if your new driver owns the car, she should ask to go out or leave a note if no one is home as a courtesy. Some form of communication is necessary, ensuring you always have a means of contacting each other in an emergency. When your daughter does have the privilege of driving a car to visit her boyfriend's house, you can certainly determine a different curfew than she has for a party or with a group of friends. You need to follow what you believe. If you believe that 11:30 p.m. is too late for her to be at her boyfriend's house, then it is. Be clear that going out is a privilege and each night's privilege depends on the previous night's responsible behavior of making curfew. Tell your daughter that there may be exceptions where a movie may end at 11:00 or 11:30, but in general, you will allow her to go visit his home until 10:00 p.m. Tell her that you are not comfortable with her visiting any later than that. The next time he visits your home, sit them down together, explaining you care deeply about her reputation and you do not want her at his home past 10:00 p.m. Then ask him if he understands and respects your decision.

You can set the standard for her appearance as well. Understand that your daughter's role models in print and TV are provocative. However, what she sees in advertising is unacceptable for your town and for you. When she is older, on her own, she may wear what she likes. For now, she will have to cover it up, pull it down, or return it. Clearly explain what she may and may not show. Set clothing boundaries by having a discussion sitting near the closet, removing clothing that you do not approve of. Warn her that, if she buys provocative things, she may have to return them, so keep the tags on! You might tell her that the girls who show all are the ones

---

33  *The First Three Years and Beyond*, 36.

who do not have enough inside their head or their heart to win over a boy's attention. The bottom line is that, while she lives under your roof, you have the right and responsibility to raise her the way you feel it is appropriate. Too many parents avoid going toe-to-toe with their teen because they don't want to deal with confrontation or explosive verbal exchanges. You have not mentioned her overall temperament, so I have no idea of what you are up against. However, I do know that you sound like a loving dad who wants only the best for his girl.

Parents of preteen and young teenage girls might consider reading Dr. Mary Pipher's *Reviving Ophelia*, a wonderful book about raising a daughter with today's challenges.

*From a baby to a young lady*

*Pumpkin carving time together*

*Three generations; Eliza, Diana and BonBon*

*Ben at 13 months old, having fun in the snow*

*Ben, a confident older brother*

*Ben, dressed for success at seven years old*

*Matthew at 10 months old*

*Matthew at 12 months, ready to mow the lawn*

*Matthew, age 3. Confident and ready for preschool*

*Eliza at 12 months, eating her favorite food, watermelon*

*My 3-year-old ballerina*

*Eliza on her soccer team*

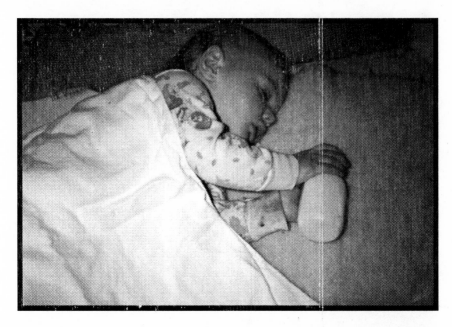

*Sleeping baby Ben, who found his bottle of water in his bear's lap*

*Older brother Ben with baby Matthew*

*Two boys ready for their pony ride*

*Two boys, best friends in PJs*

*Eliza and Matthew, hanging out together*

*Although in the middle of wallpapering his bedroom, Ben woke up on his birthday morning with his room filled with balloons!*

*On vacation at the beach*

*My two boys; the best of friends*

*Benjamin, Eliza and Matthew on the swim team together,*
*breaking records and winning medals*

*Eliza helping me set a special holiday table*

*Matthew, Eliza, and Ben (left to right) then and*

*now, Benjamin, Eliza and Matthew in Central Park*

# Schedules and Routines

## Introduction: Success Starts with a Schedule

Schedules, routines, and consistency—these three little words are so powerful for many successful families but often sound somewhat boring or rigid to parents who prefer to wing it, be flexible, go with the flow, or let their child set the pace. Unfortunately, very often, those children have difficulty at bedtime or in the morning following routines or directions. Children raised without routine or consistency can feel lost, as they do not know what to expect or when to expect it. Routine is a security blanket for a child. When a child does the same thing over and over, he learns how to master the skill and complete the activity faster than another child who comes and goes or kicks and screams due to irregular, intermittent, inconsistent exposure. Children raised with consistency and routine are often more compliant than those without because they have been raised with boundaries and schedules, understanding and processing the expectations. They are often more successful in social and academic situations, as they are more confident and have better internal self-regulation skills and higher self-esteem.

Setting up a schedule and determining your most effective routine can be simple when you break it down into the small activities that you want your child to complete. Getting your child into a bedtime routine is less stressful for everyone when you eliminate crying, pleading, and endless reasons to get out of bed. Once you have determined what the routine is to be, then develop a photo schedule book for him to follow. Be consistent with your direction and your positive recognition (verbal praise with a comforting touch) for compliant behavior. A morning routine can be set up in the same way, with photos for each expected activity (get dressed, eat breakfast, brush teeth, and such), providing your child with visual clues and the incentive of some free time before school. An after-school homework routine can be put into place by gathering all the "tools of the trade" (pencils, erasers, crayons, and so forth) into one basket with the incentive of, "When work is complete, then it is playtime!" As long as you provide the rules, review the schedule, remain consistent, and provide incentives, you can help your child to be successful and stay right on schedule.

This chapter provides specific steps to set up a bedtime schedule and a morning routine using personalized photos of your child. You will also read about how to help your child gain success with a homework routine. If you have a child who lags behind with everything or is never ready to get out the door, then read about how to set a timer to learn how to be right on time!

## Right on Schedule

Mornings can be stressful for everyone when you have a child who battles every step of the way. He will not dress and refuses to brush, and you find him in his pajamas watching television fifteen minutes before the bus is due. One child can spin an entire family out of control, making others late and causing chaos. Then there is the dreaded bedtime routine, the resistance to turn off the television, take a bath, and get into pajamas, and the never-ending requests for extra stories, snacks, or a drink of water.

I've worked with many families with young children who had no routine in place. Children thrive on routine. When there is a routine, they know what to expect, and they know what is expected of them. To help your child learn a consistent routine, develop a photo schedule book with picture cues on each page, showing a child as he completes his routine. This will keep him on track and minimize parental stress or nagging. The photo schedule book has proven successful time and time again for two-and-a-half- through eight-year-olds who absolutely love it. They buy in because it is all about them!

- **Getting started.** Write a detailed list of absolutely everything your child does to prepare for bed. Include packing up a backpack, putting away toys, taking off clothes, dropping them in the hamper, taking a bath, drying off, hanging up the towel, choosing/trying on clothes for tomorrow, eating a healthy snack, taking dishes to the sink, brushing teeth, having story time, and taking time for hugs, kisses, prayers, and lights out. Morning routines should be just as detailed and include making the bed (at least pulling the covers up), brushing hair and teeth, putting the toothpaste cap on, and so forth. Photos of every movement will make this photo schedule book so successful.

- **Take the photos.** Tell your child that you are making him a special "All about Me" book and you will be taking pictures of him moving through his morning and nighttime routines. He can pose, or just catch him being candid. After developing the photos, review them together, and talk about how pearly white his teeth look after brushing or how well he hung up his towel after his bath. Choose a nighttime (pajama) photo for the front cover, so he can identify his bedtime routine. For the morning routine, flip the book over and upside down and place a cover picture of him with his backpack, ready to go!

- **Load and go!** Purchase a small, pocket-sized photo album with clear plastic covers. Engage your child when filling his schedule book, empowering him with some scheduling decisions. When encouraged to make some decisions, he will likely participate with enthusiasm. Help him to physically slide the photos into his book, bedtime from front to back. Load the morning schedule upside down, from back to front. He will have two personalized schedule books, all in one!

## Training

The more time you spend training with patience and enjoying the routine, the more comfortable he will be with that routine. His comfort will translate into increased independence, which means minimized nagging and yelling. As you teach him to use his book, follow along with his routine by asking, "What's next in your book?" He needs to become comfortable with turning pages and completing a task without your saying, "Go brush your teeth." Your job is only to provide prompts and encouragement as he trains for greater independence. Tremendous enthusiasm should be given for his attempts and successes. Depending upon your child's age and capabilities, it may be only a matter of weeks before your only directive is, "Grab your book, and let me know if you need any help!"

*A Few Extra Tips*

This photo schedule book has been successful with many families who have taken the time to train their child to use it. Yelling and nagging are eliminated, children remain engaged with photos of themselves, and everyone starts his day as organized, calm, and ready to go. Try it. You will love it!

- Be sure to take a picture of your child after he has gone to sleep. Do not have him fake it. Children love to see what they look like when they are asleep, so authentic photos need to fill his book.

- Allow morning television or computer time only after your child is dressed, has completed his routine, and has placed his coat and backpack by the door.

- Keep a schedule book always next to your child's bed so there's no chance of losing it.

## Timing Is Everything

Do you have difficulty getting your child up and out in the morning? Do you tell him time and again to get his jacket on, but the bus arrives before he is ready? You can eliminate morning stress, rushing, and yelling by teaching your child to respond to the sound of a timer. However, first you need to be the one who responds to the timer, to model the new behavior you will teach.

Years ago, some parents contacted me. They were unable to get their four-year-old to the table for a meal, out of the backyard from playing, off the playground when it was time to leave, or into the bathtub before bed. No matter what activity he was doing, he was never ready or willing to transition to the next activity. He begged for just a few more minutes or flat-out refused to move. His parents indicated that they wanted to take him to Disney World, but since they could not get him off from the swing set in their own backyard, they had no hope of traveling with him.

I provided a training process in which the parents would set a timer for small tasks they needed to do. They set a timer for themselves about five to seven times per day, within earshot and visual range of their child. To begin, set the timer for ten minutes, and when the timer goes off, say out loud, "Well, it's time for me to fold the laundry." Set the timer again, and when it goes off , say, "Time for me to bring in the mail ... Time for me to start to make dinner ... Time for me to call Grandma." The more often your child sees you responding immediately to a timer, the more familiar he will become with that routine. After you have set a timer for about a week, for all the activities and chores you planned to accomplish anyway, set the timer for your child so he can respond to it. It is very important that the first few times you set the timer for a child, you offer an activity he just cannot resist, saying, "Hey, the timer just went off, and it's time to go to the park ... It's time to bake some cookies ... It's time to go fishing!"

When your child gets up and races to the door with shoes and a jacket, provide immediate praise. Get up and go, and give a verbal praise of, "I'm so proud of how you got ready when the timer went off!" Include a gentle, connective, physical touch to reward your child for responding to the timer. After several days of success and praise, transition the activity to something that is more of a chore or responsibility. When the timer goes off, let him know, "It's time to help me peel the potatoes for dinner ... It's time to take your bath. Do you want bubbles or no bubbles tonight?" Always praise your child, and use a connective touch when he responds immediately.

The family I mentioned and many others to follow have had great success with using a timer. One dad told me he forgot his pocket timer at home, so when it was time to leave the park, his son asked him to say "ding-ding-ding," just like the timer. He did, and his son happily got in the car. Another parent told me she left her timer at home but used her car alarm beeper as a signal, and her daughter willingly left the park. That first family did train their son to respond to a timer and were able to travel to Disney World for a memorable vacation with their inexpensive pocket timer in hand. Start timing yourself now to get ready for the morning rush.

## School Success

Sleep is critical for everyone to function well, so start a consistent bedtime routine several weeks before the first day of school. The amount of sleep your child receives will determine his ability to think, reason, and learn. The amount of sleep your child receives directly impacts social skills and academic learning. Tired, cranky children do not function well. Get your child on board with a nighttime routine that you can develop together. Take photos of your child completing his exact routine (bath, PJs, brush teeth, and such), or list them, helping your child draw pictures for visual cues. Action photos (of himself or his own personalized drawings) will help him become invested in his routine. If late-night adventures have filled summer nights, begin going to bed ten minutes earlier every other night until you reach an appropriate bedtime.

Prepare the night before. Minimize chaos. Increase your child's independence as well as his self-confidence by teaching him how to get ready for the next day. Preparation always minimizes stress. A stressed child is less able to focus on his work. The following is a checklist to be completed in the evening:

- Help your child prepare his lunch the night before. Empower him by allowing him to choose healthy items, and place napkins, drinks, and fruits in his own lunch bag.

- Help your child to choose items for his breakfast the night before. Let him arrange his cereal, bowl, spoon, glass, and cup on the table at night. Fill a small pitcher with milk, and place it on a lower shelf of the refrigerator so he can pour easily.

- Choose school clothes the night before. Check the weather forecast together for stormy or sunny reports. Empower your child by allowing some clothing choices. Have him try on his choices to be sure he is comfortable. Help him lay everything out so he is ready to go.

- Check his backpack together for homework or notes from the teacher. Fill out forms, and complete all work the night before. Teach him to put everything carefully into his backpack, and place it by the door.

School success means getting all work done in the afternoon or evening before earning privileges such as TV or games. Putting off assignments can cause subtle anxiety and make starting homework even more difficult.

In the morning:

- Prepare a morning schedule board or photo schedule book with simple pictures of his routine. Ask him what he needs to do before school so he comes up with the routine and is more involved. Ask him if he would like to get dressed or eat breakfast first. Should he brush teeth before or after breakfast?

- If TV is permitted before school, make it a privilege, something he can earn after he is dressed and completely ready.

- Play a game of Beat the Clock by setting a timer for ten minutes for each task. Be certain to recognize each task that has been accomplished. "Wow! I can't believe how your teeth sparkle!" Or you can say, "You did a great job pulling on that shirt." Everything you recognize with kind words or a gentle touch will continue each day.

- Keep mornings calm and quiet. Minimize yelling throughout the house. Take the time to get up and go to see if your child needs help or encouragement. If he is frustrated, provide empathy. "That shirt can be so tough to get on. It looks like you're figuring it out. Want some help?"

A rested child has a routine and feels prepared. He will be more successful than a tired child who has had an emotionally chaotic morning. Your attitude sets the tone. Effort, careful planning, lots of patience, and consistency can make the difference between simply surviving each morning or starting a successful day at school.

## Homework Success

Setting the standard for homework at the very beginning of the school year will help your child understand your expectations as well as the importance you place on his schoolwork. A few very important factors should be in place when setting your child up for successful work periods: consistency with routine and expectation, tool readiness, and your presence and support.

Prior to developing a routine, you need to determine the best time for your child to be successful with his work each day. Even if you are in the middle of the school year, it is never too late to help your child get into a successful homework routine. To determine a homework schedule, consider your child's age and after-school activities. Some parents feel their young child needs the opportunity to play after school, to run off energy after sitting all day. Those children then eat dinner and hit the books before bed. For some, that schedule may work. For others, it is not optimal for success, as fatigue and frustration set in near the end of the day, making it difficult to focus on work. Also, consider that, while playing outside is a great burn-off, the lingering thought of homework can dampen a child's play. Consider providing a healthy snack after school while completing homework, with the incentive of playtime after homework. A child will often excel if a parent is near, providing encouragement, guidance, and a healthful, energy-boosting snack to carry him through until dinner. After-school activities will ultimately determine your child's daily homework schedule, but most children are successful when they are on a schedule and understand your expectations. Schedules can vary from day to day depending on extracurricular activities. In which case, a weekly schedule can be put into place.

A schedule board, dry erase board, or calendar is helpful visuals for a child to maintain consistency. For example, karate lessons are on Monday and Wednesday until 6:00 p.m. and then schedule dinner, homework, a bath, and bed. On those evenings, your support is critical to ensure that your child completes his work, even though he may be tired. On alternate days when he gets home earlier in the afternoon, homework time can be regularly scheduled before play for optimal focus. So many children are successful with their rigorous schedules because structure, consistency, and support have been built into their routine.

It can be very helpful for a young child to have a homework basket at the ready, with all the necessary tools for success with any homework project. These include pens, pencils, an eraser, ruler, calculator, crayons or colored pencils, tape, glue, extra paper, and so forth. A homework tool basket eliminates frustration and wasted time in searching for materials. It also adds some excitement when new, decorative pencils or other materials are added as a surprise to his basket.

Lots of parents report that their younger child is a distraction, so they cannot help their older one with homework, as they are constantly quieting or entertaining the younger one. In that case, place simple workbooks, activity books, or coloring books in a homework basket, just for your little one. Younger children feel important and love a scheduled opportunity to do their work. That will allow you to sit at the table and help with homework while teaching your younger one the importance of work time. Make the decision to spend homework time with your child, whether you are close by preparing dinner, folding laundry, or sitting at the table writing bills. Your child receives your physical presence as emotional support, providing help and encouragement, which can eliminate hours of frustrating complaints, such as "I can't do this, this is too hard, and I don't understand this!" By being there, teaching him how to work in an organized manner and being prepared with all the tools he needs to complete his work, you are building his self-confidence and teaching him to work in a structured manner. Those early experiences will be the scaffolding for how he approaches homework for years to come.

# Dear Diana

*Parenting on the Same Page*

Dear Diana, I'm married with one child, a nine-year-old-boy with ADHD. I'm also a special ed coordinator, working about fifty hours a week. I leave for work before my son is really awake, and I am home long after he gets home from school. This leaves the majority of before- and after- school care to my husband and his mother, who drops off our son and picks him up from school.

I feel like I'm the only person who cares about his grades and the only person who enforces rules. He has begun missing homework frequently. He has two hours before I pick him up from my mother-in-law's house. She doesn't make him do his homework. I've asked her to do so several times over, but the other day, she said, "He was good so I didn't make him do his homework." When he finally gets home at four thirty, he is in no frame of mind to work, so getting him to do it sometimes takes until bedtime. Dad is little help. If I have an appointment after work and Dad is in charge, he doesn't review our son's planner to be certain work is done. If I don't ride him about getting work done, no one does. This, of course, makes me the "mean" parent. It has led to arguments and stress. How do I get the others to understand how important this is? How can one consistent parent make up for the inconsistency of others?

Dear Mom, Your background in education serves you well. You understand the importance of providing structure and support for your son. Your motherly instincts are on the mark, with your attempts to get everyone on board to help your son achieve to his best ability. Parenting on the same page is very important.

- **Make a responsible plan.** It is impossible to force others to do what you want them to do, even when it is the right thing to do. Perhaps you could get both Grandma and Dad to support a structured homework plan by expressing your concerns. Do this outside of the moment, not at four thirty when nobody has taken responsibility and everyone is defensive. Determine a time to talk about the importance of homework assignments being completed, what it takes to get them completed, and why they are not being completed now. Perhaps Grandma just wants to be a doting grandma, or maybe she does not understand the work and cannot help, so she lets it go. It is no wonder "he's so good." He has learned that, when he behaves, he does not have to do his homework. Ask Grandma if she is willing to provide a quiet spot for him, help him set out all of his work, and help him get started on his assignments. Determine a reasonable amount of time for him to work on homework at Grandma's house each day before he may play. Routine and consistency bring success. Ask your husband if he will help to complete assignments so all work is finished by dinner and you can all relax together.

- **Taking responsibility.** I truly believe that, no matter what disability or difficulty a child is facing, he can become effective by taking responsibility for his own behavior. Learning to take responsibility promotes forward thinking and increases self-confidence. Right now, your son does not have to take any responsibility for this chaos. He can blame Grandma. ("Grandma said I didn't have to!") He can blame Dad (for not checking or making him do any work), leaving the rest of the night's chaos to be your fault, as "the enforcer." Tell your son that he will now be responsible to start his homework at Grandma's house, even if Grandma doesn't make him. Tell him he will need to complete as much as he can, with or without her help. Offer several incentives (a ticket or token) for all efforts, with multiple tickets for each completed assignment. Decide together what the tickets can earn, such as having a friend over during the weekend, a family outing, or a board game with you or Dad.
- **Reaching your goal.** Involve everyone in helping to identify the problems that need to be overcome, and ask everyone to offer a solution. When people talk about a problem, they can often understand each other's concerns, resolve their conflict, and achieve a successful outcome.

# 8

# Sleep

## Introduction: Sweet Dreams, My Little One

There is nothing quite as beautiful as a sleeping baby. Watching a baby sleep can be so peaceful as their little mouths move so gently. Their bodies startle and then relax as they move throughout their sleep.[34] As infants grow into babyhood, then into toddlerhood, and later into their preschool years, some parents may develop a greater difficulty in putting their child to sleep and/or keeping him asleep. So many wonderful sleep reference books provide a myriad of styles and a wealth of knowledge regarding the necessary amounts of sleep according to the age of your child and a variety of ways to get through the night. Dr. Richard Ferber and Dr. Sears are leaders in the medical profession who provide sleep training strategies, backed by their peers and other medical professionals. Over the many years I have worked with parents, I have not come across one mom or dad who felt it was easy or simple to train a child to sleep. None ever enjoyed hearing a child cry. Listening to a baby or toddler cry can be devastating for some parents, while it is exceptionally stressful for others. It goes against our nature to allow a child to cry, to allow him to feel distressed without comfort, when he could easily be picked up and soothed back to sleep. And there lies the problem.

Children learn to fall asleep in the manner in which we teach them. Some parents go for car rides, while some parents rock their babies and toddlers to sleep for years. Some parents pat their child's back until he drifts off; others lie down with their toddlers until they fall asleep. Still

---

34  *Touchpoints: The Essential Reference,* 59.

others provide continuous bottles or pacifiers, replacing them in their mouths throughout the night. As we know, children learn what they live. Therefore, the sleep pattern training that you initiate will be the one that continues until you are ready to retrain your child out of one pattern and into a new one.[35] Training a child out of a comfortable pattern can be difficult, as he may cry from confusion and distress. This chapter contains many articles regarding the need for sleep, the amount of sleep needed, and how to get your child to sleep.

## Consistent Sleep

Sleep is a beautiful thing. It directly affects the functioning level of our minds and bodies. Without it, serious physiological difficulties can develop, including diabetes, obesity, attention deficits, increased blood pressure, headaches, impairment of overall ability, and compromised immune systems. Adequate sleep for children is absolutely critical, as it determines their emotional temperament as well as their ability to absorb and retain information to increase functioning in all areas of development.[36]

Many families find it difficult to get their children to sleep in their own bed. Some parents drive around in a car to get them to sleep. Some allow their kids to sleep in their bed for years, putting up with cramped space and an occasional foot in the face because it is just too difficult to get their child to sleep in his own bed. Some parents simply give up, allowing their child to fall asleep on a couch because removing him from a TV into a bedroom is a struggle and just too much effort. Children need to learn how to soothe themselves to sleep, finding comfort in their own space with their favorite things surrounding them. It is a gift to your child when you take the time to teach him how to follow a bedtime routine and to fall asleep in his own bed. Children learn from repetition, and they can quickly learn an evening routine by doing the same thing over and over. On the other hand, if a parent continually allows his child to fall asleep in his bed or on the couch, that is how that child will learn to fall asleep. As children grow older, it is much more difficult to break old habits. A battle is inevitable when you are ready for your child to go to his own bed, but he still wants to fall asleep in front of the TV.

Every parent knows that getting a child to sleep can take tremendous patience and great effort until his child is able to learn the routine of the

---

35 *Touchpoints: The Essential Reference*, 94.
36 *The Big Book of Parenting Solutions*, 586.

evening. It is a gift to your child and yourself to implement a relaxed bedtime routine so your child will have the benefit of increased sleep time. Include story time in your routine each night, no matter how young your baby is, as that shared quiet time will nurture so many parts of your child's emotional and intellectual well-being. When you believe in yourself and the process of the routine and remain consistent with your response, you can easily train your child to fall asleep in his own bed. Structured routines provide emotional security for a child. He will learn what to expect, when to expect it, and, just as importantly, what is expected of him. Give your child the gift of a bedtime routine with plenty of sleep. You'll all sleep a little better.

## No More Bedtime Struggles

Providing a quiet, structured, consistent routine for your child's bedtime is the key to getting everyone in bed on time without tears. Dr. Richard Ferber, director of the Center for Pediatric Sleep Disorders in Boston, recommends that children ages one to two years old should get thirteen or more hours of sleep every day. Children two through eight need from ten to twelve hours of sleep per day, and adolescents are recommended to get from eight to nine hours of sleep each night.[37] The proper amount of sleep is critical for children. Tired children can become unreasonable and have continuous meltdowns. While we sleep, our organs regenerate, and cells rebuild. It is important that you provide the maximum opportunity for your child to succeed with the proper amount of rest. It is also important to reduce external stimulation at least an hour before bed, as that can cause your child's brain to remain alert. External stimulation includes exercise, rough play, TV, video games, bright lighting, loud noise, and high-level conversation, to name a few. Change your routine, eliminate external brain stimulation, and see if your child is able to fall asleep with fewer struggles. A quiet routine will help your child learn to fall asleep in his own bed to get a full night of restful sleep.

## Getting into a Routine

Consistency can be a very difficult skill to master. Giving in can be so much easier for that moment. However, in the long run, consistency is truly a gift to a child. Young, concrete thinkers thrive on sameness and repetition to learn and grow. Deciding to provide a structured bedtime

---

37 *Solve Your Child's Sleep Problems*, 19.

routine is the first step. Based on your child's age, determine an appropriate time for lights out and then work backward to develop your routine. List all the things that need to be done before bed. Once you make this decision, do not fall back into inconsistency. Inconsistency sends a mixed message, causing confusion and chaos.

## Making It Easier

For a young child who does not require a night feeding but may still wake for a bottle, you can provide multiple small bottles of water in his crib. A photo schedule book may help your child learn to follow and enjoy his bedtime routine. It is easily used with three to eight-year-olds who can follow picture prompts. Read details of how to develop and implement a photo schedule book in Schedules and Routines. Visit www.yourperfectchild.com, and click the Shop with Us tab to order a blank photo schedule book for your child.

Provide a bedtime basket for an older child, which he can fill with favorite books to look at by himself after lights out. Each night, allow him to choose several favorites or even a chapter book, and review the rules together for clarity. Remind him that he may have the privilege of looking through books as long as he remains quietly in bed. Provide a small flashlight or glow sticks in the basket, and have him repeat the rules. Another soothing addition to an older child's bedroom is a lava lamp, which provides a dimly lit slow, calming visual motion. Some children love the idea of a dream catcher, which they can make themselves and hang in their window. Other children feel a sense of protection with an angel decoration or an enlarged family photo. I painted my son's ceiling a pale blue sky with clouds and applied a galaxy of (stick-on) glow-in-the-dark stars with planets. Quiet, classical music or sounds of nature (rain or the ocean) also are very relaxing and help little minds to easily drift off into dreamland.

Whatever your preference, be sure to provide your child with a calming environment and a regular routine for relaxed and successful bedtimes.

## Step-by-Step Training

It can be so frustrating for a parent whose child simply will not go to bed or stay there. It is a difficult decision to do something about it rather than to continue thinking, "He will grow out of this." Your child's physical health and emotional stability depend on his sleep. When you are ready, empower yourself with books and videos about sleep training. Talk to your pediatrician, and reach out to friends who have been successful. Put your supports in place, and find someone to call when your child is crying or testing the limits. Ask your support person to keep you on track. Always remain close to offer support and eliminate evenings filled with yelling and chaos.

Once in bed, your child will most likely test you with requests for water or the bathroom, or make statements that he cannot sleep. This is where the real work begins, so you need to remember why you decided to develop a bedtime routine. A well-rested child displays less misbehavior and will function better in all areas, including in school. Try to remember this as your child negotiates, gets out of bed, or tries to push you to your limit. Be prepared to dedicate an entire evening to bedtime training for the first few nights. Much less time will be required once your child is comfortable with the routine. According to Dr. Richard Ferber, director of the Center for Pediatric Sleep Disorders in Boston, most children learn to follow a bedtime routine within seven nights, although many children will learn to soothe themselves to sleep within three nights.[38]

Remember that your child has nothing to lose by negotiating or crying for an hour or more. He only stands to win if you give in, teaching him that you cannot withstand his tears. When your child gets out of bed, calmly and lovingly say, "It's time for bed now." Do not respond to requests or pleading if your child has already had that last drink and has used the bathroom. If you feel he may truly need to use the bathroom, take him by the hand, keep the lights low, do not talk to him, and do not make eye contact. Assist him as he goes in and comes out of the bathroom. Without further words, walk your child back to bed, and tuck him in. He will probably pop right back out of his bed to see if you will reengage. Without verbal communication, eye contact, or moans and groans from you, move him back to his bed, and cover him up. Sit near the door, where he can see you, but do not face him. Just be there to place him back into bed without communication. It is critical that you do not respond or reengage with any behaviors or remarks. Quietly and calmly place your child back into his bed. I have worked late into the night, sitting in bedroom doorways with moms, providing the encouragement they needed to train their child to remain in their bed. It takes inner strength and patience, so be prepared. A little six-year-old that I worked with got out of her bed one hundred and eighty-seven times the first night, fifty-one times the second night, and three times the third night. After that, she learned her routine and learned

---

38 *Solve Your Child's Sleep Problems*, 79.

to go to sleep in her own bed. Her parents were delighted that she was better behaved during the day because she was so well rested. They were also delighted to have their evenings back!

## Time Changes

*"Fall Back"*

"Falling back" with an extra hour of sleep for an adult is indescribable. However, unless you slowly adjust your child's sleep clock, the time change may wreak havoc with early morning wakeups and bedtime or nap disturbances. Do not be surprised if your child's sleep patterns are out of sorts a bit or even a lot during a change in daylight savings time. Help your child to rewire by transitioning with small, incremental bedtime adjustments so he will be ready when it is time to turn the clocks back.

If you have less than a week to transition your child to the time change, beginning tonight, start bedtime routines fifteen minutes later. Continue to start bedtime by fifteen minutes later every other night until you reach your desired bedtime with the time change. In other words, if bedtime routines usually start at seven o'clock with a bath, get him into the tub tonight at seven fifteen. Continue with your exact bedtime routine without changing or eliminating any activities. Lights out should be a bit later every other night.

If you become frustrated with the effort that is required to change your child's bedtime, do not show it. The definition of transition is learning to move with ease from one topic or place to another with seamless effort. That is the goal, which is important to remember whenever you become frustrated. Take a breath, and try to enjoy reading bedtime stories a half hour later than usual, even if you are missing part or all of your favorite television show. Relax and enjoy the transition, knowing you are helping your child adjust to a time change. The more effort you put into his bedtime routine, the more successful your child will be in regulating his sleep clock. Throughout this process, if you sense he is becoming overly tired, start a warm bath or offer a quiet story. Do not offer games or TV time. Quiet bedtime activities, stories, songs, and a review of the day are relaxing and comforting and will provide an ideal atmosphere for a successful transition.

Some children who experience troubled sleep, those who have difficulty falling asleep, those who do not stay asleep, and those who get up early in the morning may do so for a variety of reasons. Some of those reasons include internal biological clocks (like a rooster), being a light sleeper (where household noise will wake him), too much sleep during the day (naps too long or too late in the day), or stress. Yes, children experience stress from peer pressure, bullying, household chaos, and mismanagement or a misunderstanding of their behaviors. The following are some helpful hints to minimize sleeping difficulties:

- Light sleepers can be successful sleepers with white noise or quiet, consistent noise as a background throughout sleep. Minimize household noise as much as possible, and be aware of loud, jarring noises. Play classical music that has been developed for young children, or turn on a fan for a quiet hum.

- Naptime should be individualized, but the length should rarely exceed three o'clock in the afternoon. Your child needs time to wake up, explore, eat dinner, and then wind down for the start of his bedtime routine around seven.

- Alleviating stress can be the focus for each evening in the bath or even in bed, as you review your child's day with all the wonderful things he did.

Develop an easy, stress-free schedule, and stick to it. Decide what time your child should be in bed with lights out. Now, work backward. Twenty minutes before lights out, read stories to him in his bed. Just before that, squirt toothpaste on his toothbrush, and sing a song while he brushes. Just before that, you dry him off with a soft towel and help him into his PJs. Before that, he was in the tub, relaxing in the warm water and playing with the bubbles. In many cases, it is a very easy transition. A quiet, stress-free, structured bedtime routine with minimal chaos for at least an hour before bed will set your child up for success and give him the sleep he needs (ten to twelve hours). It will also give you the time you need in the evenings to recharge yourself for tomorrow.

## "Spring Ahead"

As the warmth and beauty of a long anticipated spring approaches, we let our minds wander to visions of longer, warmer days where our children can finally get outside and run! Another sign of spring is daylight savings time. Springing forward means losing an hour of sleep, which can disrupt a child's internal clock. It can take days or even weeks to adjust due to a lack of sleep, leading to cranky temperaments and meltdowns.[39] Although it is not too much of a problem for adults, losing an hour of sleep from one day to the next is quite a leap for a child who goes to bed on Saturday night at his usual eight o'clock but is expected to fall asleep on Sunday night at seven according to his internal clock. With a good plan and a little effort, you can keep your child right on schedule. Help him transition with success and go to bed at his usual time rather than an hour later than usual for nights on end after the clocks change.

When possible, plan ahead. A slow transition may take about three weeks to get your child to bed an hour earlier than usual. Start bedtime routines ten minutes earlier, beginning immediately, and move it back by ten minutes every third night until you reach your desired bedtime. For example, if bedtime routines usually start at seven o'clock with a bath, get your child into the tub at six fifty tonight. Move consistently through your exact bedtime routine without changing or eliminating any activities. Keep bedtime snacks, brushing teeth, stories, and songs all before lights out. There is no need for a lot of discussion regarding time changes. However, if your child can tell time or questions his new bedtime, tell him you are slowly changing his internal clock. If favorite TV shows present an issue, offer to record the show, which can be viewed the next day after school and homework are complete, provided bedtime goes well the previous evening. Going to bed on time is the requirement for tomorrow's reward. Just remember that you are the parent. Remain patient and consistent with your plan.

Many pediatricians agree it is easier to adjust an internal clock with a slow, incremental transition. A very consistent bedtime routine will help to slowly transition your child to sleep one hour earlier over the next few weeks. Understand that you are adjusting your child's internal clock, so when he says that he is not tired, offer another bedtime story rather than an extra game time or TV time. Quiet bedtime activities, stories, songs, and a review of the day are relaxing and comforting. Those quiet activities will provide an ideal atmosphere for his long-term transition. Some children do experience trouble falling asleep, some may not be able to remain asleep, and some may get up early in the morning before they have had their ten to twelve hours. Possible causes include being a light sleeper, too much sleep during the day, or stress. As previously mentioned, children can experience

---

39  www.babyzone.com/toddler/article/daylight-savings-time

stress from peer pressure, bullying, household chaos, major changes in routine, no routine, or a misunderstanding of their behaviors. Be mindful of these triggers so you can look for, minimize, and eliminate the causes.

Implement the same steps as described previously. Develop a stress-free schedule, and maintain it with consistency. Determine the time you would like for your child to be in bed, and work backward. For example, twenty minutes before you turn out the lights, read stories in his bed. Fifteen minutes before that, help him into his PJs. Just before PJs, he should have been relaxing in the tub, playing in the bubbles.

Make it your priority to enjoy a quiet bedtime routine with your child. It is a time for reassurance and love. In most cases, providing a quiet, stress-free, structured routine one hour before bedtime will help your child to fall asleep and remain asleep. Offer a special bedtime basket filled with a few favorite books. Suggest that your child quietly enjoy these books by himself with his night light turned on. Your efforts will pay off, and you will be ready for daylight savings time.

# Dear Diana

*Questions and Answers for Sleep Training*

Dear Diana, I am a grandfather of a twenty-two-month-old boy. I do not remember it being this hard to raise children. My daughter is a stay-at-home, thirty-four-year-old mom who thought that raising a child would not be too hard since millions of people do it! Her biggest issue is the lack of sleep she is getting due to sleep issues with her child. She and I have read all of the books from Ferber to Sears, to "total cry it out," and nothing seems to work with this child. He is very headstrong. She has tried letting him cry, but after about fifteen minutes, he starts banging his head on the crib and hitting his knees against the slats. His knees seem to be bruised quite frequently. After about fifteen minutes of banging, she goes in, gives comfort, tells him it is sleepy time, and then walks back out. She does not take him out of the crib. He cries for another fifteen to twenty minutes. He actually kept this up for one and a half hours one night. So, here are my questions:

**Q:** I am an educator with thirty-seven years of teaching grades four through eight, so I am somewhat familiar with the idea of consistency. Consistency surely makes life easier for students, teachers, and parents, but I am still battling the idea of nature versus nurture. My wife (grandmother) thinks she is to blame for his poor sleep habits since she would walk and/or rock our grandson and bottle-feed him until he fell asleep in her arms. My daughter continued doing this, but now it seems the child cannot soothe himself to sleep. I hope my wife did not give some wrong information since this technique worked with our two girls. I really feel that there are some kids who are easier to raise than others. Just like in the classroom, some children learn easier than others. All children are not born the same, but which has more bearing on this sleep issue, nature or nurture?

**A:** Nature versus nurture is so difficult to define in so many areas of child development. I agree with you that some children experience more difficulty in certain areas than others and then excel in other areas. And yes, some children are easier or more difficult to raise than others. I also believe that, if we look closely, we can determine what is troublesome for that child, problem solve through it, and remediate the troubling behavior. Sometimes, a child's behavior is a direct result of how his parent has handled a situation. Educating a parent how to retrain a child can be very successful.

When it comes to nature versus nurture, I believe it is a bit of both. Some children, teens, and adults can manage on less sleep than the typical population. However, most of us need a regular, consistent, seven to twelve hours of sleep, depending on our age. The "nurture" is where parents and educators have the opportunity to reshape, redirect, and retrain. Your wife should not feel guilty for providing tender loving care to her grandson. Your grandson is following the patterns he was taught. He was trained to fall asleep in someone's arms so he has never learned how to self-soothe. Transitioning from warm, loving arms with a bottle into a lonely crib is dramatic. It is natural for him to become upset or confused. He is using his coping skills, and he has learned that, if he cries long enough, bangs his head, and knees against the bars, he will get the attention he is looking for. He has learned that his mom will eventually return and provide comfort.

**Q:** Is there a small percentage of children who will not respond to any sleep methods? What do you do with these children?

**A:** Pediatrician Lawrence Handwork of Akron Children's Hospital encourages parents to develop a bedtime pattern, stating that all children, with the exception of those with compromised medical or neurological factors, can be trained to sleep when consistent, appropriate routines are provided. Your toddler has been trained to do what he does with certain patterns of consistent behavior that your wife and daughter provided. Change the pattern. In my experience as a teacher of children with special needs, I found that every student, no matter how delayed or disabled, was able to learn and display the skills that I taught. Children can learn to soothe themselves to sleep with consistent patterning. Believe that you can teach him how to soothe himself to sleep. As a teacher, you know that, when a child is learning a new skill, it takes much effort, complete dedication, and repetition with consistency. He may test your limits and pull out all the stops. You need to be fully ready to follow through with what you have started, or you will be sending a mixed message. If you decide it is too difficult to follow through, he will learn to cry louder and longer, knowing you will eventually give up and rescue him. This is how children learn to become headstrong.

**Q:** The procedures outlined in Dr. Richard Ferber's book, *Solve Your Child's Sleep Problems*, make sense to me, and with a little effort and consistency, they should work. But how long do you let a child cry, and how long can you let a child bang his head on a crib? Our pediatrician says he will stop banging his head on his crib bars whenever he is ready. When will that be?

**A:** Dr. Ferber's methods can be completely successful if you are willing to let your child cry for the short intervals described in his book. His method is one of reassurance every few minutes, which provides a child the opportunity to comfort himself to sleep. As you stated, it can be equally as distressing for the parent as it is for the child. I have guided many parents through the Ferber Method, providing encouragement throughout the bedtime process. Listening to a child cry is heartbreaking. It is our nature to comfort and soothe. You need to be fully prepared whenever you start a sleep training program, believing you are giving your child a gift by teaching him how to soothe himself to sleep. Many temper tantrums are driven by sleep-deprived children. Proper sleep is critical for continued brain development and appropriate social functioning. Those are just a few reasons that Dr. Ferber's method is so widely accepted, purposefully implemented, and completely successful.

Your grandson's headbanging is distressing, as it is now known that concussions and head injuries can have lasting effects on the brain. Although children have banged their heads since the beginning of time, either by accident or purposefully without injury, it would be neglectful to advise you to allow him to bang his head for your attention. Consider implementing an alternative method, described below, and redirect his headbanging while providing new patterning. Your daughter will be able to help him learn to self-regulate.

## Training, Retraining, and Patterning

When you are facing a behavior that needs to be addressed, it is best to gather everyone involved to dissect the behavior. Discuss all of the conditions that could possibly be fueling it. Questions to ask: Who puts him to bed every night? Is there consistency with the procedure, no matter who puts him to bed? Is there a nice, long, calm routine in his room to help him transition before lights out? Does he sleep through the night? If not, why not? What time does he get up in the morning? Does he take a daily nap? What time is naptime, how long does he sleep, and what time does he get up from his nap? What kind of exercise or stimulation does he get during the day? Children who are placid or watch TV for much of the day may have more energy to burn than those who attend preschool, which has structured activities or playing in the fresh air.

Developing a sleep training plan is much like developing a professional teacher's lesson plan. Start by setting your general goal, which is to have him fall asleep at an appropriate time without crying. Set your objectives:

- To teach him to accept bedtime as a time to sleep
- To teach him to accept and use a soft toy as a source of comfort to help himself fall asleep
- To be able to stay in the room until he falls asleep, providing emotional support for him without feeling guilty, but understanding that this is a training period

## A Plan That Works for Everyone

Many effective sleep plans can be put into place to train your child to go to sleep. The following is an alternative to leaving your child alone in his room, crying, and banging his head on his crib.

- Make sure everyone is on the same page and can follow through with the plan. Everyone will need to tolerate and endure some amount of crying for several nights.

145

- Choose a soft toy or blanket that your child can carry with him during the day. It will pick up his scent and provide him comfort when he is in his bed. Whenever possible, hold that blanket or stuffed toy while holding your child. Place it in your lap or under your shirt to pick up your body scent. Your scent will comfort your child when he holds it close.

- Commit to spending time in your child's room each night. Sit quietly with no eye contact or verbal exchange. Silently offer a soft toy or blanket as a redirection when you hear him get out of his bed or bang his head.

- Be certain that your child is tired when putting him to bed. Review nap patterns. Follow the three o'clock rule, which means no sleeping past three. He needs to be tired and ready for bed by seven thirty or eight.

- Prepare and use a photo schedule book of his bedtime routine. This book will engage him and help him become invested in the process. After completing his routine, goodnights can be said to favorite stuffed animals, and soft music can be played in the background. Dim or turn off the lights, and put him in his crib with hugs and kisses. Then sit in the dark, out of reach, facing away. You may find that you need to distract yourself by quietly humming a song, reading a book with a flashlight, or making a to-do list for the next day so you don't give in, provide comfort, or take him out of the crib. That would be confusing and make it more difficult for him to learn how to put himself to sleep.

The purpose of staying in his darkened room is to monitor his safety as well as convey the message that you are there and he is safe. When he bangs his head, hand him his favorite blanket or stuffed animal for comfort. Do not say anything or engage in any way. If he throws it down, offer it one more time and then walk away. No hugs, kisses, or loving words. Although your daughter may feel better when she gives a hug and says, "It's okay. You'll be okay. It's sleepy time," that engagement may be heightening his frustration, adding fuel to his fire so crying will continue for longer than it needs to. The second night, move closer to the door. Sit quietly in the dark until he falls asleep. Implement the exact same behavior as the night before so he can learn the consistency of the new pattern. Each night following, move slightly closer toward the door until you are eventually at the door. Then transition to sitting in the hallway. This may take several weeks, as it needs to be a slow transition with the exact pattern each night.

Finally, provide recognition and praise each morning, relaying how proud you are that he went to sleep so nicely last night. Bribes, stickers, and toys are not necessary, but recognition is critical, as children thrive on positive attention.

## *Additional Techniques and Strategies*

To teach my son to self-soothe and fall asleep on his own, I filled multiple four-ounce bottles with water and placed them in the lap of his big brown bear, which sat in the corner of his crib. When he cried, I moved his hand toward the bear to find one of the many bottles of water. After a few sips, he fell back to sleep. With my help, after a few nights, my son learned to find his water by himself as he reached for his bear. By placing so many bottles in his bear's lap, he could always find one easily, even in the very dim light of his room.

My second son did not attach to a soft toy, a water bottle, a pacifier, or a blanket. I knew it was important for him to attach to something for comfort, so I made a quilt.[40] Throughout the weeks it took to sew, I bundled him in the fabric and held him close to me so it would pick up our body scents, which I knew would help him to connect and attach. It provided a great comfort for many years and remains a treasured item, packed carefully in the attic.

Another alternative is to put your child to bed with his regular routine and then sit in a chair in his room for about five minutes in the dark. When you get up, if he is still awake, tell him you will be back in several minutes after you fold the laundry. Return as promised, without speaking. Sit in the chair for five more minutes. Repeat this pattern until he is asleep. Within several nights, he will fall asleep, perhaps while you are gone from the room, feeling comforted to know you will soon return.

## *Bedtime Success*

I have worked with many families over the years, providing support with one of the many routines described above. We have worked together in their homes or over the phone throughout the night. Throughout all of my experiences, I have only worked with one mom who was not able to

---

40  *Infancy: Infant, Family, and Society*, 354.

get her son to sleep, but her husband could. He followed the exact routine with success. What does that tell you?

Transition is difficult for most children, but there is almost always something to help your child become comfortable and learn a new routine. Patience, empathy, love, consistency, and endurance make up the recipe for thoughtful parenting, which will bring successful learning. We have an amazing opportunity to teach our little learners. We just have to be prepared with a stellar lesson plan and then follow through by teaching the lesson.

# 9

# Toilet Training

## Introduction: Are You Ready? Is Your Child?

Potty training can be such an exciting time. Your child has grown a little older and a little more independent. Potty training can also be a stressful time for parents who become anxious or may even develop a sense of insecurity regarding their parenting abilities. Although philosophies have come and gone regarding when or how to train, several clear indicators remain constant. So many variables determine potty training success.

Children need to be both physically and emotionally ready before being introduced to the potty. Muscle control must be developed, which you can recognize when diapers remain dry for longer periods of time. Do not push a child who is not physically capable of training with success. Night training usually occurs many months after successful daytime potty training. Consistently dry overnight diapers may indicate nighttime readiness. To help a child transition through that process, fluid intake should be monitored and minimized throughout early evening hours. Your child's maturity, along with your family environment, can be a factor in your child's emotional readiness. If a new baby is due, do not start to train your child, as regression often occurs. Provide an environment so your child feels secure and happy when attempting to use the potty. Parents who show distress with accidents can send an unspoken message of disappointment or control. Address an accident by identifying the facts of what happened. Move into the bathroom to clean up, using an even-toned voice and providing wipes and dry clothing for semi-independent changing. Showing emotion or becoming upset may trigger your child's desire to control when or how he will be trained. Emotional control can transition into intentional urination or dangerous bowel withholding. These behaviors often require focused remediation or medical attention.

The following chapter provides information regarding when to start potty training and how to follow through with success. Circumstances that might cause resistance or regression are provided with helpful strategies to minimize power struggles. Every child is unique, so training one child may be a very different experience than training another. Whether you have a toddler who is ready to train or an older preschool child who refuses to leave the comfort of his pull-ups, you will find answers to your questions, alleviate your concerns, and learn to develop a game plan for successful training.

## Common Toilet Training Questions

Parents have many questions and concerns regarding potty training. The following are some common ones:

**Q:** What is the right age to begin training my child?

**A:** Age does not determine the best time to start training, although certain holding muscles do not develop before twenty to twenty-six months. Family dynamics, birth order, and emotional readiness are significant markers to consider.

**Q:** What are the signs that my child is ready to train?

**A:** Training can be successful when a child remains dry for longer periods, recognizes he is either wet or dirty, displays uncomfortability, or requests to be changed. Successful training requires physical muscle control as well as emotional readiness. When your child shows interest in the potty and willingly sits with success, successful training should occur.

**Q:** What is the worst thing that can happen if I try to force my child to train before he is ready?

**A:** You cannot force your child to become potty trained. When a parent is overly anxious, talks about it often, or provides a lot of attention to the matter, the child will sense it and may make unhealthy decisions. Some children intentionally wet themselves to see the frustration, anger, or disappointment. Some children go on the potty to see excitement. They can withhold bowels for days to get their parent to back off from potty training. Bowel withholding can become a medical danger. Your pediatrician should be contacted immediately if you see indications of extremely hard, painful, or irregular bowels. If you try to force training before your child is ready, the training period will often take much longer. Children have the ultimate control over their training, so both you and your child need to be really ready.

**Q:** Are all potty seats the same?

**A:** Some potty seats sit on the floor, some insert into the toilet seat, some help a child to step up, and some even play music when they are being filled. These should be chosen based on your child's age and physical size. It helps to introduce your child to a portable ring or a potty seat for travel purposes.

**Q:** Do girls train differently than boys?

**A:** It is beneficial for boys to learn to stand. Boys who are trained solely to sit may be teased in a preschool setting where groups of children travel to the bathroom together. Peer pressure or humiliation can cause regression or refusal. Sitting and standing are different experiences, so it is helpful for boys to become comfortable with both.

**Q:** Does the same approach work for all children?

**A:** What works for one child may not be successful with another. Having a sense of your child's readiness or resistance is the key. In many cases, it may be easier to train your second child because he may want to emulate his older sibling. Older siblings should encourage the younger trainee.[41] Also, a child who is referred to as "the baby" may enjoy that role and may not show an interest in training.

**Q:** How should I handle naps and bedtime with pull-ups or diapers?

**A:** Staying dry throughout the night usually occurs several months after daytime success. Liquids taken in after early evening hours play a big role. Limiting evening liquids and monitoring bathtub faucet drinking can be

---

41 *Infancy: Infant, Family, and Society*, 404.

difficult and upsetting. It is better not to mention this limit and offer small sips instead of a full cup.

**Q:** How do I handle using the potty when we are not home?

**A:** Several strategies can be successful, depending upon where your child is with his training. It is always important to be mindful of the last time your child used the potty. Plan for errands to be short. A house rule should be initiated so everyone always uses the bathroom before leaving the house. Keep a travel bag in your car, stocked with several changes of clothing, underwear, plastic bags, socks, wipes, pull-ups or diapers, and a potty ring, if your child is comfortable using one. If you have a larger vehicle, you might keep a travel potty in the back for emergencies. This immediate, private space can provide peace of mind to a toddler. The more relaxed and prepared you are, the more successful your child will be. Bad experiences typically cause regression.

**Q:** Why do some children train and then regress?

**A:** Children regress for a variety of reasons. It is very common for an older sibling to regress when a new baby arrives because the baby receives so much attention. Accidents require attention, and toddlers often regress for that attention. When this happens, remain indifferent, and help your child to clean himself, saying very little. Giving sympathy or excuses or showing disappointment or anger will provide attention to the unwanted behavior. Try not to become upset or reward the behavior with emotion or excuses. Remain indifferent, providing as little attention as possible to the event and giving your child no positive reinforcement. Other causes for regression include upsetting experiences or difficult transitions, such as a death in the family, a divorce, or moving.

**Q:** What should I do when, no matter what I try, my child just will not use the potty?

**A:** Stop trying. This almost always occurs when a child senses his parent's desperation. You cannot force him to go, so he really does have total control. In this case, it is best to pull back. Work hard to show no emotion, as if it really doesn't matter to you. Stop asking if he needs to go, and stop taking him to the bathroom routinely. Tell your child you can see that he is not interested in using the potty, so you are putting it away for now. Do not say, "You're not ready." For a greater effect with faster results, go back to diapers, not pull-ups. When you change diapers, say nothing, with no talking, songs, or smiles. Nothing. Do not display anger, frustration, or disappointment. Be mindful of your body language and facial expressions. In other words, give no attention, neither negative nor positive. Chances are that, within days or a week, he will ask to use the potty because he will want to receive the attention he was getting when it was out. When you do reintroduce the potty, try a different approach without pushing or urging. Remain indifferent, and always have him clean himself (with minimal assistance from you) when accidents occur. When he is successful, say, "You must be so proud of yourself," as opposed to "I'm so proud of you." Teach your child to be proud of his accomplishments.

**Q:** What should I do when accidents continue to occur with my older child who should already be trained?

**A:** Check with your pediatrician to eliminate any medical or sensory processing concerns. Once cleared, approach this as a behavior that requires an intervention. Refer to this as soiling, not accidents, as they are not accidents. They are purposeful with the intent of gaining attention. Give no attention, negative or positive. Accompany him to the bathroom without words, and show him how to change himself. Be sure to teach him with kindness, as this is intentional teaching, not a punishment. Without your attention and with having to learn how to change himself, the behavior should be eliminated within a few weeks.

## Developing a Potty Training Plan

Potty training can be distressing for parents if their child becomes empowered. However, that does not mean you should be apprehensive about starting to train. Quite the opposite. Train your child with a thoughtful plan. Understand where your child is in the process of training by considering his emotional readiness and his physical capability. When you decide to train, be ready to move forward, providing an unspoken expectation of success with your potty training plan. Be sure that you feel fully confident, have read material on the topic, and have spoken to others who have completed the process. Ask about their difficulties as well as their successes. The following are simple steps to take when beginning to train:

- Place a potty seat in the bathroom, teaching your child that a bathroom is the place to go. Kitchens and family rooms may be convenient, but they may not be conducive to going. It is also very helpful to teach a clear message that we go in the bathroom.

- Take your child to the potty throughout the day, simply saying, "We are going to the bathroom now." Use the bathroom after drinks, before and after baths, before meals, and before going out on errands. Make it a common experience, always keeping conversation light and showing indifference if he does not go.

- Talk about diapers as being uncomfortable, smelly, and causing hurtful rashes. Name friends and family who use the potty/bathroom. Avoid saying, "Diapers are for babies," as some young children may want to be babied or taken care of and therefore interpret your statement as a reason to stay in diapers. Avoid saying, "You are such a big boy, and big boys do not use diapers." This implies he should be ready and may cause him to feel guilt if he is not. Guilt does not teach. Guilt can provoke feelings of anger or resentment, providing a reason to wet or withhold.

- Read potty books, and choose fun, colorful underwear as an incentive and basis for conversation.

- Help your child shake his dirty diaper or underwear into the toilet to be flushed, showing him where it goes.

- Prompt how to flush.

## A Few Tips

- Always change your child in the bathroom so he can become familiar and comfortable with the area.

- Invite your child each time you use the bathroom so he learns that this is what people do.

- Fill a special, brightly colored basket with wipes, diapers, pull-ups, underwear, socks, sweat pants, potty books, and favorite theme books to be placed near the potty. Offering choices of which underwear to wear (or even a pull-up) can help in the transition. When a child feels he is in control, he is often more successful.

• For a boy who is ready to stand at the toilet, suggest using a piece of toilet paper as a target. Words like, "Ready, aim, fire!" can make it fun and therefore successful.

## Dear Diana

*Problems with Toilet Training*

I recently received two letters with similar concerns, so I am addressing them together.

*Dear Diana,* I have a lovely, intelligent three-and-a-half-year-old grandson. He was very easy to potty train and seldom has accidents, but he will not poop in the pot. I am worried that his parents have now put too much emphasis on it because he will go into another room and poop in his pants. They have tried rewards, withholding things, and all manner of that, but he will say, "I will do it when I am older." My daughter is very frustrated and does not know what else to do. Concerned Grandmother

*Dear Diana,* I have a four-year-old son who is refusing to have a bowel movement on the potty. For several years, we have had problems with him holding his bowels. He takes Miralax and fiber gummies on a daily basis. He will hold a BM until he is put in a pull-up at night or go in his underwear during the day. I have asked him why he won't go on the potty, and he says, "I don't want to." Whenever we find that he is trying to go in his pants, we try to convince him to go sit on the potty. We have tried everything! We have given rewards for the few times he has gone on the potty, and when he goes in his pants, we take a favorite toy and put it in a time-out on top of our fridge for the day. Neither reward nor time-out is working. My mother keeps reassuring me that he will eventually do it, but my husband and I are really frustrated. My son's pediatrician says this is common for children to hold BMs during potty training, especially if they've had a painful bowel movement episode. We would appreciate any advice or help on this matter. Desperate Mom

*Dear Grandma and Desperate Mom,* Thank you both for writing on this topic, as I am certain that so many others share your concerns. Children have total control over three bodily functions: eating, sleeping, and toileting. We cannot force a child to ingest food, fall asleep, or produce results on the toilet. When a child is coaxed, bribed, or begged, he gains a sense of control. A child will usually continue with that behavior until he no longer receives the attention or loses his audience. In most cases, neither positives (bribery) nor negatives (punishments, yelling, or taking away) will change the behavior because nothing is as important as the power he holds with his body.

Serious medical effects can evolve if a child refuses to eat or drink, causing malnutrition or dehydration. Toileting empowerment can evolve into bowel withholding, a physical control often leading to constipation and sometimes requiring hospitalization for elimination. Bowel withholding can cause impacting or pressure on organs. Hiding in a corner to eliminate is fairly common. If humiliated while using a quiet corner, a child may begin to withhold. A thorough discussion with your pediatrician is critical to eliminate constipation as a factor. Many parents struggle with toilet training because so many variables can cause problems. With tremendous dedication and lots of love, you can learn to implement a very successful strategy that is individualized for your child.

Some children have a difficult time using a toilet because they feel a piece of them is being flushed away. When you begin to potty train, prompt your child to flush the contents of either his diaper or the potty chair pot into the toilet. This will help develop an understanding of where things go. A big toilet can be frightening because some children have a fear of falling in. Children do not necessarily view their bowels as we do. Some toddlers smear (or in their minds, paint) all over their cribs or walls. When they see the expression of horror, they do not understand. Older children may use fecal smearing as a cry for help or even as a weapon, threatening to smear if they do not get their way. The attention a child receives can determine how he will choose to eliminate. Minimize your attention, including discussions or changing an older child who is fully capable of changing himself. Eliminate threats and bribery. Teach your child to be comfortable with flushing, and encourage him to take ownership of his bodily functions.

Several years ago, I was a guest on a television program, presenting strategies to increase toileting success. The following is a very methodical, successful intervention. Toilet training implementation requires consistency, dedication, and an expression of your confidence through your voice and actions. There is no going back once you begin. If you are inconsistent or show frustration, your child may gain control and regress to soiling.

Help your child to become ready by providing a bathroom basket filled with wipes, liquid soap, hand sanitizer, washcloth, hand towel, clean underwear, a plastic bag for soiled underwear, clean socks, and clean pants. Show him the items, one by one, explaining their usage. Your tone of voice is very important. In a kind, teaching voice, say that he seems uncomfortable using the toilet and prefers to go in his pants. Do not use the word "accident." He is not having accidents, but rather, he is making a choice. Tell him that you are going to allow him to change himself from now on. Explain that, although you will always be there to help, you will not be changing him anymore. Avoid conversations such as, "What if I can't do it? What if I need your help?" A simple reply could be, "I have confidence in you, and I will help you whenever you need help."

Initially, he may test you by crying and say he cannot clean himself. If he cries, provide encouragement saying, "Sure you can. I showed you the other day. I will help you." Then lead him into the bathroom. If he has soiled himself behind the couch and continues to play, provide the facts. Kindly say that you can tell he soiled his pants and he will get a hurtful rash if he sits in it. Ask him if he would like your help in the bathroom. If he declines, do not show emotion, beg, or bribe. Instead, think of an incentive. For example, explain that lunch will be ready or he may play outside as soon as he is clean. Prompt him to let you know if he wants your help. Stick to it, and move on. When he does want or need something, tell him you can get it for him when he is clean, using the words "when" and "then." For example, say, "When you change into clean underwear, then you can go on the swings." Remember, your tone of voice as well as your emotional control will impact his success.

Once in the bathroom, minimize your physical help. Quietly provide one- to three-word verbal directions with hand-over-hand assistance, if necessary. When he is finished, praise him with one simple sentence of, "You must be so proud of yourself," using a gentle, loving touch. The next time he soils himself, help less, but always be near for support. Over time, your child will tire of cleaning and changing himself as long as he is not receiving any attention for it. This thoughtful, incremental behavioral training has been successful for the many families with whom I have worked. This process will require multiple attempts in a consistent environment.

With your help, he can learn the process, take responsibility, and become comfortable using the toilet. Minimized attention, your confidence in his ability, and your control over your emotions, intonation, and actions will be the scaffolding for his complete success.

# 10

# Fears

## Introduction: Building Emotional Security

Childhood fears are common throughout developing years as children observe, experience, and engage in new activities and events. Their experiences shape their level of success with attempts to try, do, or become part of new situations. It is typical for some children to feel uncomfortable or uncertain when presented with new information or events. They may be incapable of verbally identifying fears. They may act upon them and express their distress in a variety of ways. Their behavior may seem ridiculous, or maddening, as one mom put it, when they cry endlessly, whine, or cling relentlessly due to some fear that seems unfounded. When a child accelerates into a full-blown meltdown, a parent can do very little to help him de-escalate, except perhaps to hold him quietly. The most important action a parent can take is to understand that his child is uncomfortable. Thoughtfully accept it, and thoughtfully acknowledge it. When a child feels heard and understood, he may feel more secure, develop an increased trust in the situation, and learn to become more comfortable in that environment.

New situations can cause distress, anxiety, or fear. Slow introductions are helpful when small bits of information are provided in an upbeat but relaxed tone of voice. Too much information or information provided too far in advance can also provoke anxiety. Some typical fears might include being left with a sitter, going to bed in a dark room, attending large, loud family events, the start of a new school year, attending a new class, or being left in an unfamiliar environment. Children moving from one town or school to another can have anxious moments. Even teenagers entering high school can become anxious of the unknown. New situations and change are difficult for everyone. No matter what the age or anxiety, it is better addressed with empathy and understanding than impatience and anger.

Telling your child that there is no reason to be afraid or that he shouldn't be upset will not resolve his fear. Do not discount your child's fears. As stated above, it can be very helpful when you acknowledge a fear with a physical connection, a hug or a back rub, which provides nonverbal communication of unconditional love and understanding. Simply saying, "It seems you are thinking about meeting new friends at school," can sometimes start a simple conversation. Remember that the words you choose, the pace of your words, and the intonation of your voice are all signals. Your child is watching and listening for nonverbal clues. Most children respond exceptionally well to techniques designed to diminish anxiety. Provide the following strategies in a relaxing, fun environment outside of the time of the presenting fear:

- Provide a worry box and encourage your child to write or draw his worries, talk to you about it, drop it in the box, and let it go.

- Provide a daily worry time so your child can safely and consistently express his concerns, and communicate more regularly about things that are distressing for him.

- Teach him to run up and down the stairs to release endorphins, increase oxygen flow, and distract him from the presenting fear. Use his age as a guide for how many stair runs he completes, for example, five years old equals five times up.

- Post a feelings faces board in a prominent place where everyone in the family can place a magnet on a face to express his current feeling. This provides exposure and an awareness of the many emotions that everyone experiences.

- Ask him to think of his most favorite time, such as a vacation where he was digging in the sand, a party with all his cousins, the day you built a swing set, and so forth. Tell him you will send him off to that favorite time whenever he seems distressed. Let him know that you will help him "change the channel" and move into that fun time with a secret code. Develop your secret code together.

- Teach him how to reset himself with a relaxation technique. This is best taught during when he is completely relaxed, perhaps before going to bed. Refer to it as a "four, five, six, reset!" where he breathes in for four seconds, holds for five seconds, and breathes out for six seconds. Again, this stimulates oxygen flow and teaches him to transition his thoughts from a place of fear to a place of concentration.

- Teach body relaxation, which can be fun to practice while lying in bed after stories. Have him straighten his arms, tighten his fists, stiffen his legs, point his toes, grit his teeth, and, lastly, hold his breath. Now, one at a time, reverse. Breathe, ungrit teeth, unflex toes, relax legs, loosen fists, bend arms, and roll head around to loosen neck muscles. That is a great one for everyone!

## Stranger Anxiety

As holidays approach and extended families gather, many relatives will see great-grandchildren, grandchildren, nieces, nephews, and cousins for the first time in a long time. It is a most wonderful and exciting time to gather. However, for a young child, it can be distressing or overwhelming. Loud noises, big crowds, overstimulating and unfamiliar environments, and a lack of routine can contribute to a child's distress. Consider your child's emotional regulation when planning events and family gatherings.

Stranger anxiety can be exhibited in a young child from as early as eight months, as children younger than that generally accept unfamiliar faces and allow others to hold and soothe them.[42] However, just a few months of maturity can make quite a difference for a child, and even family members may be viewed as strangers if they have not had consistent exposure. Stranger anxiety can continue into toddlerhood. It can ignite a higher level of anxiety or mistrust and manifest in different ways if it is dismissed or ignored. Some children may withdraw, either physically or emotionally, while others may become quiet observers. Some children may scream loudly, cling to, or hide behind a parent. Some may bite or hit in self-defense as their only way of communicating their distress. It may be helpful to explain to others that your child is experiencing stranger anxiety, and although he seems a bit shy, he may warm up if he is not pushed. Hold your child, providing security, while others approach. Invite others to gently touch your child, speaking softly while you are holding him.[43] If your child has a favorite soft toy or blanket, invite the friend or family

---

42  *Ages and Stages*, 25.
43  *Touchpoints: The Essential Reference*, 101.

member to offer it to your child. The scent of his special cuddle toy will provide comfort.

In advance of a family event, collect or request close-up photos of all family members, placing them into a small, durable, plastic-covered photo album for your child to carry and own. I put together just such a book for my first child, Benjamin, born twenty-nine years ago on Thanksgiving, and we referred to it as his family flip book. He held his own, personalized picture book, some family close-ups, and some photos of family members holding him. We flipped through those photos often, especially before he visited with them. I integrated his sense of smell by having a small cloth handkerchief doused with my mom's perfume and another with my dad's cologne. When he looked at his Grandma Bon Bon's picture, I handed him the handkerchief with her perfume so he could associate her scent with her picture. The book went everywhere with him, and he was able to associate the photos with those familiar family members in his book.

It can be distressing to friends or family when a child will not warm up to them. With understanding, patience, and a few behavioral strategies, you can minimize your child's anxiety and help him to accept love and affection from close friends and family.

## The Circle of Life

Several weeks ago, I telephoned a friend, and although she answered my call, she said she would call back because she was at the checkout counter of the pet store, purchasing a goldfish for her daughter. When she called back, I asked why she was buying another goldfish since her daughter already had one. Well, apparently the fish had not been feeling well, and it was floating upside down in the fishbowl. My friend said she was ready to have her counter space back, but her husband thought it would be better to replace the fish while Katie was napping. So, again I asked, "Why?" That would have been a perfect opportunity to teach Katie about life cycles, beginnings and endings, loss and grieving. However, Katie's dad wanted to protect her joyous spirit and spare her from an emotional upset, for which he is admired.

Teaching children about death and dying is never easy. Children are so innocent and look at the world around them with interest, excitement, and amazement. Perhaps exposing a child to the concept of death is difficult because it is so very difficult for us. When relatives are very ill and pass on, we are often told it is better this way. They are out of pain. Nevertheless, their passing often leaves us with deep pain in our own hearts. Teaching a life cycle can be an educational experience for a young child, as you explore an ant nest, watching for the queen ant and her workers, or look for cocoons and caterpillars that evolve into butterflies. This exploration of nature is also a great opportunity to teach your child that all creatures, big and small, have homes and families. Those lessons may actually help your child learn to be kind to all those in the animal kingdom instead of attempting to step on ants and spiders.

If you are interested in teaching life cycles but not the outdoor nature type, purchase some inexpensive, colorful guppies, which are low maintenance and as hardy as goldfish. The bonus is that guppies birth live babies, which is fascinating. I recall sharing my dresser with a tank of guppies. I was responsible for changing the water, daily feedings, and saving my allowance for fresh plants to oxygenate the water. If a fish tank is too much, consider buying a single goldfish or a beautiful betta for your child to care for.

We had many family pets as my children were growing up, which helped them learn about responsibility and the cycle of life. We had a wonderful family dog, Sophie; a rescued greyhound; a black cat; multiple rabbits; saltwater and freshwater fish; hermit crabs; a guinea pig; hamsters; Shelly the turtle; a hedgehog; an iguana; and a flying gecko. Although I was not passionate about some, each pet found its way into our home and into our hearts. As each pet lived out its life, my children loved and cared for it. When life cycles ended, we all gathered together to hold a memorial, burying most of them in our wooded backyard. They learned that this was all part of the process. As difficult as any ending may be, it is helpful for a child to learn about life as it comes and goes. The poet Alfred Lord Tennyson said, "'Tis better to have loved and lost, than never to have loved at all."[44]

Katie is happy with her new goldfish, unknowing it was replaced. However, the next time her fish floats, both parents said they will be ready to help her learn about the circle of life.

## Preschool Anxiety

Eventually, it will be time to prepare your child for a transition from home to school, a place filled with new and exciting experiences. Some children find it difficult to leave home, as they are completely comfortable with

---

44  www.brainyquote.com/quotes/quotes/a/alfredlord153702.htm

their surroundings, Mom or Dad, their own toys, and familiar playmates. Preparing your child with the understanding of possible separation anxiety will help him to be much more successful during those first days of school.

Separation anxiety is well known to all early childhood educators. They understand it can be just as difficult for some parents to separate and let go as it is for their child. Attitude and actions have a great deal of influence on a child's reactions and can determine the success of the separation experience.[45] It is a whole new world with new toys to explore, friends to make, games to play, foods to taste, books to read, and stories to share. This is the beginning of your child's school career, independence is gained, self-confidence is ignited, information is processed, and social skills are developed. It is where children learn to take turns, share, wait, listen, and explore. For some, it can be a sensory overload and somewhat overwhelming.

Crying and clinging are a typical display of anxiety or separation difficulty for a young child. Look at these first few days through the eyes of your child. Consider what it feels like for him to go somewhere new, meet new people, and follow new rules, alone. Be patient and tolerant of emotions. Ask "wh" questions, such as these: What did you like best? Who is your new friend? If your child does cry or cling, rely on the experience of his teacher to engage him in classroom activities.

You can prepare your child for separation by talking, showing, and going.

- **Talking.** Lots of conversation regarding school-based activities will help your child to prepare emotionally. Descriptions of glue and paint projects, as well as birthday or holiday celebration parties, will help him imagine the fun to come.

- **Showing.** Show your child new toys, games, and books that he might use in his new classroom. Head to the library or the educational section of your local toy store. The purpose of the outing is to explore, not purchase. Pique his interest by telling him you are going to look at things he may be able to play with every day in his new classroom.

- **Going.** An adventure trip to your child's new school will spark interest and excitement as well as provide comfort and minimize anxiety during the first few days. Walk around the school, find his

---

45 *Ages and Stages*, 26.

classroom, and share a snack on the bench of the playground. Stop by the main office to meet a friendly face who will help your child connect.

## Things to Remember

- Always say good-bye and tell your child when you will be back. Some parents feel it is easier to sneak away because they do not want their child to cry or do not want to leave while he is crying. Sneaking away creates mistrust. Your child will learn to trust you when you come back each day. Most children stop crying minutes after their parent leaves. Teach your child that he can trust you, that you will come back right after lunch or at the end of every day.

- Do not give in or get angry when your child cries. Definitely do not take him out of school. Parents who remove their crying child will actually teach their child that he can go home with Mommy when he cries. It will also make going to school the next day much more difficult for both of you.

- Keep your expectations high for your child. Let him know he can be anyone and do anything. Spark his imagination, and let him know that everyone is there for him at school. It is where he will learn to become whatever he wants to be.

# 11

# Siblings and Friends

## Introduction: My Brother, My Sister, My Best Friend

Siblings can be the best of friends or not. Siblings can stand by each other through thick and thin, encourage each other, teach each other, and spend time with each other, bonding a true, lifelong friendship. Siblings are also known to fight like cats and dogs, tattle on each other, physically hurt each other, or leverage themselves by telling each other's secrets. The expectation and environment provided by their parents determine much of how siblings relate to each other. If teasing and tattling or pushing and fighting are tolerated, then that will be how those siblings interact. If they are taught how and expected to show acts of kindness toward each other, then they will display those skills. Some parents say they have tried and tried to get their children to be kind to each other, but they just won't listen or stop arguing. If a sibling bond is your focus, you can provide the skills they need for a successful relationship. Specific steps will encourage kind, thoughtful behavior, and there are very clear ways to nurture family unity.

If your children are already at odds with each other, gather them around the table with a piece of paper and a crayon for each. Have them trace and color their two joining handprints to symbolize friendship, unity, and a helping hand. Cut them out, and have your child tape it on your refrigerator. Next, have them trace just one hand next to a picture of a face, symbolizing a hand hitting a face. Have them draw an X through that picture to symbolize "no hitting." Include zero tolerance for yelling or saying hurtful words in your house rules. Have each child tell you about his picture and the new rule. This is called "teaching outside of the moment," and it is very effective. Yelling at children while they are fighting will not teach the new rule.

Unless it is easily determined that one child hit and the other did not retaliate, let your children know that, if you see them fighting, both will be disciplined because it takes two to fight. Discuss what their natural consequence will be if they forget or make the choice to fight. A natural consequence might be to have each child think of an act of kindness toward the other (clean his room, be his butler and get him things he wants for an hour, and so forth). Have your children think of acts of kindness that they would want to have done for them and write them down. When the fighting is over, the acts of kindness begin. Provide clear expectations for behavior to eliminate all gray areas, to eliminate arguing, fighting, and yelling.

To increase a sibling bond, introduce an act of kindness jar by adding a marble each time you see a child perform a random act of kindness toward anyone. Examples include holding a door for someone, offering to help outside with the yard chores, offering to take out the garbage, offering to help a sibling get dressed, reading or playing a game with a sibling, offering to help a sibling with homework, or whatever! Whenever an offer to help is made, that child may place a marble in the jar. When the jar is filled, the entire family celebrates with a trip to the zoo, a banana split party, a family bowling outing, and so forth. As you eat your ice cream or enjoy your outing, remind everyone about the wonderful acts of kindness that earned the reward. You will be reinforcing thoughtful acts while improving sibling relationships.

Read more in this chapter about how to increase sibling bonds throughout each day because siblings can be the best of friends.

## Getting Rid of the Rivalry

When I was a teenager, I learned how powerful a strong sibling relationship could be. My closest friend and her sister were the best of friends. They trusted, protected, and constantly showed acts of kindness toward each other. I decided that, when I had children, I would make it my mission to help them become the best of friends.

Sibling rivalry has often been a topic of concern with families. Siblings compete for attention. They tease, argue, instigate, and blame. They hit and say hurtful things to keep each other in their place. Some allow it, feeling this is typical sibling behavior. I wanted more for my three children, and I found the following strategies to be very successful in promoting healthy, loving relationships.

- **Build a team.** When talking to a child about a sibling, refer to the other as "your brother" or "your sister" rather than using a name. Continually referencing with "your sister" or "your brother" sends a strong familial message. It helps siblings attach to each other, work together as a family unit, and learn to be team players rather than fight to be the star of the team. Some families refer lovingly to their child as "the baby" long into toddlerhood. Babies are babied and receive lots of attention, something every child wants. Identifying one child as "the baby" may build jealousy or a great deal of resentment between siblings. A child's perception is their reality.

- **Set the stage.** When my three children were young, I continually told each one how much the other sibling other missed him throughout the day. I would say, "Your brother is going to love to see your picture when he comes home from school." When picking one up from preschool, I would say, "Your sister missed you so much and cannot wait to show you her picture!" My mantra to all three was that friends come and go, but you will always have your siblings. I also set them up for successful playtimes so the time they spent together was positive. I encouraged sharing and cooperation with each activity and monitored them closely so I could intervene quickly before arguments started.

- **Promote acts of kindness.** When you inspire children to participate in acts of kindness, it increases their self-confidence, which reduces their need to display misbehaviors for negative attention. Children do not naturally hold a door for a stranger, pick up something that someone else has dropped, or help a sibling zip a jacket. However, a little parental encouragement can help a child to feel those successes. I worked closely with three children, ages six through nine years, who were in constant competition, arguing often and functioning as individuals rather than as a team. I suggested their parents describe various acts of kindness that could earn an incentive of five minutes. When thirty minutes were accumulated, they could cash them in for an activity with a parent. Activities included baking cookies, going for a walk or bike ride, and playing a board game. Spending time with a parent is the ultimate reward. The child who cashed in was able to choose the activity, either alone with a parent, or invite the sibling(s) to join. Including siblings can empower a child to feel very special as well as foster closer relationships. Some might feel that earning minutes for acts of kindness is an unnecessary form of bribery. However, babies are born as self-centered beings. Just ask any two-year-old to share! Children need to be taught. They learn how to share and be kind through their experiences. It is definitely worth the effort to nurture your children's relationships so they can become the best of friends. Everyone wins.

I worked with a mom who said her three-year-old daughter was always grumpy in the morning and her seven-year-old son seemed to enjoy causing trouble with his sister. We talked about the amount of sleep they were both getting, bedtime routines, sleeping through the night, and their morning routine. Deficiency in any one of those factors can affect a child's behavior and therefore change the dynamics of the morning routine for the entire family. Everything seemed to be in place.

When I asked about specific behaviors that caused concern, Mom said that when her daughter sat at the counter to eat her breakfast, her brother climbed on his stool to sit next to her. She whined and cried because she did not want him sitting there. Mom said she told her son to move, to eat at the kitchen table because his sister wanted to be left alone. She said he usually ate at the table for a while but then returned to the counter, bothering his sister, asking questions, and attempting to sit with her. His sister screamed for him to get away, and Mom said she ended up yelling at him for taunting her. In no time at all, everyone was in a bad mood first thing in the morning. She said it was a vicious cycle, and it had been going on for a long time. It had become a habit. I provided a favorite phrase, "Nothing changes if nothing changes." I explained that, if she looked closely at what was happening, she could see what she could do differently in order to change the dynamics. I also offered her the definition of insanity, which is doing the same thing over and over and expecting a different result.

I asked Mom why she was directing her son away from the counter to the table instead of serving them both at the counter for breakfast. She thought I was kidding because her daughter screamed, carried on, and caused chaos when her brother came near her. She said it was just easier to send him to the table because her daughter got so upset. She said the problem was that he just kept coming back to cause trouble. I wondered if she realized that she had been allowing and actually enabling her daughter to have a tantrum in the mornings. Initially, Mom referred to her son as the troublemaker when, in reality, it was her sweet little three-year-old daughter who needed to be removed and retrained. She was the one who needed to learn to calmly eat breakfast at the counter with her brother.

Very often, parents ask the well-behaved sibling to give in, give it up, or get out of the way simply because it is easier than confronting an out-of-control child. However, giving in to that out-of-control child will reinforce and empower the child, communicating it is an acceptable way to behave. In this case, the little girl manipulated who sat at the counter by her behavior. It also is important to note that Mom saw her son as the troublemaker when he was set up for failure from the beginning. It is not fair or reasonable to have one child constantly make concessions for another child's bad behavior. Although Mom had never viewed the situation from that perspective, I encouraged her to address the problem with a "say less, do more" strategy.

"Say less and do more" means not talking about what you are going to do. Just do it. Mom was prompted to invite her son to the counter for breakfast. When her daughter began screaming, she removed her from her stool and told her that she would be invited back for breakfast when she could join her brother quietly. I reminded Mom that her daughter's inappropriate behavior had been part of a family dynamics for quite a while, warning that retraining may require multiple trials before everyone sat together successfully. I urged her not to give in but rather be consistent in what she said and did every morning.

Within a few days, Mom successfully created a new environment. The family sat together at the counter for breakfast, and all enjoyed pancakes! If you're having a problem with your child, take a step back, pull it apart, develop a strategy, and determine a game plan where everyone wins.

## Successful Playdates

Teaching a young child how to play nicely requires practice with other children of the same age. Formal programs and playgroups provide the scaffolding for learning social skills needed to develop lasting friendships. Some parents may invite another child to play at their home, assuming the two young children will know how to interact appropriately. An unstructured environment can lead to arguing, hitting, crying, and the end of a playdate with little ones who lack skills for sharing, compromise, and communication. Set your child up for success by following simple guidelines for safe, successful playdates with friends. Before a playdate, explain the rules:

- **Friends share.** "Your friend is a guest, so he chooses the first activity, and then you will be able to choose. Will that be hard to play with trucks first, even though you might want to play with your trains? Do you want to try? If you try but have a meltdown, I will choose the games to play. Can you tell me the rule about who gets to choose first?"

- **One toy at a time.** "You can only play together with one toy at a time, so there is not a big mess to clean up in the end. I will check on you to see if you need help cleaning up. We will tell your friend that the toys that come out must be put away."

- **If it's out, we share it.** "Are there special toys that you do not want to share with your friend? If so, we will put them away. Otherwise, anything that is out is to be shared."

- **Your friend is our guest.** "We want your friend to be comfortable and happy. You need to use your manners by sharing, speaking nicely, and keeping your hands to yourself. If you have a problem or become upset, come to me so I can help you. Do not push, hit, or yell at your friend. We want him to come back and play another day."

*The Process*

Invite one child to your home for a limited, two-hour time period, perhaps on a weekend when both parents are home. Plan the playdate as if you are a preschool teacher.[46] Ask your child which types of activities he might like to do with his friend. Offer some suggestions, allowing him to make choices so he can take ownership to the activities and be more successful with sharing.

- **Activity 1 (15–20 minutes):** Provide the children with an opportunity to prepare a snack (mixing brownies, slicing refrigerator roll cookies with a plastic knife, preparing instant pudding, mixing a fruit salad, and so forth). Let the snack sit as the friends go to unstructured play.

---

46  *Ages and Stages,* 144.

- **Activity 2 (20–30 minutes):** Take the children to the toys they may use for unstructured play. Explain the four rules. Allow them play without your direction for a limited time. With a close ear, check on them in ten minutes, remarking on how well they are playing and sharing together.

- **Activity 3 (10 minutes):** Break for the snack they prepared.

- **Activity 4 (20–30 minutes):** Move to the next activity, which your child may choose.

- **Activity 5 (5 minutes):** Cleanup time! Sing a song, play a CD, and accompany them as you designate responsibilities. "You put all the cars away in the bin while your friend puts the blocks in the tub. I will pick up all the train tracks. Ready? 1, 2, 3, go!"

- **Activity 6 (20–30 minutes):** Have a craft on hand (model airplanes or woodworking projects) that can be purchased inexpensively at a craft store for a few dollars. Keep the children engaged with an interesting craft while they talk together.

When children enjoy time together with structured activities, they learn the skills needed to be successful playmates. This process is also easily implemented for siblings to increase bonding and strengthen sibling relationships.

# Dear Diana

*Improving Sibling Relationships*

Dear Diana, My daughter is two and a half, and my son just turned one. My daughter gets very frustrated with her brother. He always wants to be right next to her, playing with her toys, opening the door when she uses the bathroom, and so forth. She gets upset, yells, and pushes him down. I know that two-year-olds are very possessive ("Mine!"), but how can I help her learn to share? Is she not developmentally ready for the concept? What should I do when she pushes him down? How should I handle him when he pulls her hair? (He loves the reaction from her!) Mom of Two

*Dear Mom of Two,* It is wonderful that your son displays his love for his sister. His interactions and responses are very age appropriate. He is learning from her with everything she does. Pulling her hair and following her around are his way of engaging with her. You can change the outcome (her negative response of pushing, yelling, and screaming "mine!") by focusing on ways to increase her role as her brother's encouraging teacher, role model, or coach.

My three children attended a Montessori school, and when my son was five, he was given the opportunity to read simple stories to younger nonreaders. The younger children thought he was amazing, so his self-confidence soared, his attention-seeking behaviors decreased, and he developed leadership skills. Helping to tie shoes, offering to carry items, or holding a door for a younger one are simple examples of behaviors to be nurtured and encouraged. In your situation, your daughter needs to feel that she a very important, positive role model. Respect your daughter's concerns, and set boundaries for your son when she wants privacy. Respond in the exact same manner with consistency so both children will learn quickly. First, go to your daughter, saying, "There is no reason to scream. Just ask for my help." Next, remove your son, using the word "privacy." Remove him to another location each time he approaches her in the bathroom.

When your son pulls hair, go to him first. Remove him from the immediate area, saying, "You may not pull hair." Place him down within eyesight, and go quickly to your daughter. Soothe her, and give her plenty of attention. Children behave for a response or reaction. When your son does not get that fun screaming reaction from his sister, his hair pulling will decrease. When he is ready to reengage, carry him to her, place his hand on her hair, and say, "Sorry for pulling hair." Although he does not have those language skills, he will learn to apologize by doing. When your daughter becomes angry or pushes him down, repeat the same process, using the same intervention. Address her unacceptable behavior with a verbal correction, and provide plenty of attention to your son.

Sharing is difficult for many, many children. It is a concept that needs to be taught repeatedly, so put on your preschool teaching hat. Establish a house rule of, "If it's out, we share it." That means your daughter can play with special, higher-level items when her brother is napping or is fully engaged in another activity. Focus on facilitating activities they can do together each day, such as a wagon ride or stroller walk, where she pulls or pushes her brother. Interpret for your daughter, explaining what he is trying to do or say. Praise all levels of kindness, saying, "Look, your brother wants to share his cookie with you! He loves you so much." You can definitely improve their relationship by nurturing the goodness in them both.

# Dear Diana

*Older Siblings and a New Baby*

*Dear Diana,* I have a four-and-a-half-year-old son, a two-and-a-half-year-old daughter, and a three-week-old baby boy. My older two children really seem to love their little baby brother. However, I find myself repeating, "Don't touch him. Please stop. You're going to hurt him." I want my older children to bond with their baby brother and enjoy being big brother and big sister. However, they can be so rough with him, and newborns are so fragile. I do use phrases like, "Please be gentle. Like this," and I will take their hand and demonstrate for them how to be kind and gentle. I will even stroke their arm and say, "Doesn't that feel good when Mommy is gentle?" I am also trying to really praise my older children when I "catch them" being good or helpful. I have a "Catch ya being good" jar we fill with pirate coins. Both kids really like that. So I am wondering if you can offer any further suggestions for helping to ease my family through the transition of welcoming a new baby. Sincerely, Mom of Three!

*Dear Mom of Three,* Congratulations on your growing family and your commitment to building a strong, healthy sibling bond. It is difficult to watch little ones try to bond when they have no concept of how very fragile an infant is. Although they may enjoy their new baby, it is very natural for them to feel jealousy as their family positions have changed.[47] Your daughter is no longer the baby, and your four-and-a-half-year-old now has two others to share you with!

When my second child was three months old and his big brother was twenty-three months, I found our small pumpkin, which had been purchased for our new baby, in the garbage. Although always physically gentle with his baby brother, after three months of living with a crying,

---

47  *Touchpoints: The Essential Reference*, 199.

needy new baby, my older son had clearly communicated his emotions. When my daughter was born and I became a mother of three, I was given a set of glass geese, a mother and her three goslings. I found the littlest baby gosling broken on the floor, fairly confident that her older brother, who was the baby of two but had become the middle child of three, had accidentally broken it. Every family has a story of how an older child adjusts to a new baby, but it is important to remember that babies always need our vigilant monitoring as we are their only protectors.

It sounds as though you are doing a wonderful job of reminding your two children to be careful while taking their hand to gently stroke their baby brother. Try using the words "soft and gentle" repeatedly as you stroke them throughout the day or take their hand to stroke their brother. Children associate soft with a favorite stuffed toy. They are familiar with the word "soft," so use it often and whisper it softly. Eliminate "please don't" or "don't touch," as they may do those behaviors to see your reaction. Always tell them what you do want. Tell them that babies are fragile and can break. That is a concrete message for them to understand, as I am sure they have broken one of their own toys and can associate a sad feeling with the break. When you see them approach their baby brother, ask them if they would like to hold him. Provide four simple holding rules. "You may hold your brother when Mommy or Daddy give you permission, Mommy or Daddy hands your brother to you, you are sitting right next to Mommy or Daddy, and you are sure that you can be soft and gentle."

After some time, they will lose interest in holding their new baby, finding other exciting things to play with. For right now, he is new, and your two older children can get your attention, push your buttons, and get you to elevate your voice simply by being just a bit rough. Welcome your two older children with supervision, and you will find their soft side. Ask them if they would like to help change his diaper or be a go-for person for simple items. Then you can give them a pirate chip for being so helpful and continue to promote all the positives!

# 12

# Bullies

## Introduction: Time for a Change

The following is what you need to know about bullying, bullies, and being victimized or targeted by a bully. It is what you need to know to protect your child, to be certain that your child neither falls victim to nor ever becomes a part of bullying.

Bullying may be physical with poking, pushing, hitting, kicking, spitting, or literally beating up a target. Bullying may be verbal with yelling, teasing, taunting, name-calling, lying, insulting, or threatening. Bullying may be done indirectly through intentional ignoring, full exclusion, spreading rumors, telling lies, or convincing others to bully someone. Bullying can be either physical or emotional abuse, or both. It has three defining characteristics. It is deliberate, as a bully's intention is to hurt or intimidate someone. It is repeated, as a bully often targets the same victim again and again. It is a power imbalance, as a bully will choose a target that he perceives as vulnerable. Bullying affects everyone: the victim, the bully, and bystanders. The effects can be lifelong. Bullying is not a predisposition. It is neither harmless nor inevitable. Bullying is a learned behavior. It's harmful, and it is controllable. Bullying spreads if no one stops it. Bullying can be effectively stopped and completely prevented when we take steps to prevent it.[48]

So what can you do? When you see someone being bullied, do something about it. Hesitation will enable a bully to continue. Approach

---

48  www.bullyfree.com/free-resources/facts-about-bullying

and help the target by physically removing him if necessary. Your actions may change or save lives.

Bullies have been around forever, altering and damaging the lives of others. At the lowest level of bullying, there is intimidation, which, over time, causes the target to become insecure and to think less of himself. Imagine someone having the power to strip your child's self-esteem. Imagine your child falling victim to a bully. Diminishing self-esteem and causing humiliation is the very least of the damage a bully can cause. Sarcasm, a noted form of bullying, makes fun of another person, while the "jokester" (the person who was "just kidding") gets a laugh at his target's expense. Develop zero tolerance for sarcasm in your home, so that when your children hear it, they will bring it to your attention as a mean or hurtful statement. Children learn what we teach them. They learn by what they are allowed to say and to do. As parents, we have tremendous influence over whom our children will grow up to be. We are powerful, and we can end bullying by teaching our children, reporting what we see, and requesting our schools be compliant with national policy, infused lesson plans, and the implementation of annual bullyproof programming.[49]

Read more in this chapter to learn what you can do to prevent bullying.

## Zero Tolerance

Bullying is a serious issue. It intimidates, rips self-confidence, heightens anxiety, promotes fear, ignites violence, and causes death. As adults, parents, and educators, we need to do everything possible to teach zero tolerance regarding bullying.

Clinical psychologist Dr. Bobbi Beale of Child and Adolescent Behavioral Health in Canton, Ohio, reports that bullies are often those who have an inflated sense of self-worth and seek power. They do not know how to communicate, or they lash out in an attempt to be in control while keeping criticism or focus off themselves. It runs rampant among the eight- to eighteen-year-old crowd, although it certainly affects those who are both younger and older. Statistics show that bullying can occur as early as three or four years old. According to the American Medical Association, 3.7 million children have been involved in bullying.[50] Increased absenteeism is reported to be directly related to children's fears of being bullied in school. Twenty percent of students are afraid throughout much of the school day.

---

49  *How to Behave So Your Preschooler Will Too*, 263–65.
50  www.bullyfree.com/free-resources/facts-about-bullying.com

Every seven minutes, a child is bullied on an elementary playground. It is time to make some changes.[51]

## What's in It for Me?

People do things because they get something out of it. Why do bullies bully? Bullies may seek power or popularity. They may be looking for attention, or they may be jealous of their target. Bullies usually find someone who stands out in some way, which is why so many children insist on wearing clothing to look just like their friends. They can't bear the thought of standing out in a crowd because they will draw attention, which can be dangerous.

In January 2010, Phoebe Prince committed suicide. She was a beautiful, fifteen-year-old, new student in a quiet Massachusetts town. She was bullied at school and over the Internet, all until she killed herself. Her bullies faced criminal charges. There have been many more bully suicide stories in the news since 2010, and each child, tween, teen, or young adult was bullied to death.

Perhaps bullying stems from our general acceptance or participation in teasing or sarcasm. ("I was just kidding! Can't you take a joke?") The definition of teasing is to pull apart the fibers of, to annoy, to torment. Some view sarcasm as the highest form of humor. The definition of sarcasm is "a bitter cutting jest; a severe taunting, derived from the Latin meaning of ripping flesh (someone else's)." When I learned the definition of sarcasm years ago, I developed zero tolerance for it in our home. My children learned to identify it easily when they heard a sarcastic remark. Their awareness was heightened.

## Where Does It End?

We need to teach our children that all forms of bullying are unacceptable. We need to teach them how to identify it and report it. Making fun of someone is the simplest, most basic form of bullying. Standing by and watching it happen sends the message that it is acceptable. We need to teach our children to look out for their siblings, their peers, or even strangers in need, extending ourselves to others.

Many websites are dedicated to bullying. A specific child-friendly website for schools and families is http://www.stopbullying.gov/. It has

---

51  Ibid.

videos, fact sheets, activities, and topics for conversation. It also directs your specific concerns to a licensed clinician. It is up to all of us to teach children how to maintain self-esteem and handle everyday criticism. Take each opportunity to explore and validate your child's feelings while problem solving together.[52] The more you talk, the more they know. Children raised with love, empathy, and education can make a difference.

## School Bullies

Bullies have been around forever, but now they are making international news headlines as their behavior results in the deaths of others. Technology has become a deadly weapon for bullies as they send video recordings or picture messaging to cell phones or over the Internet. The ramifications of cyberbullying are so far reaching that they leave some targets to feel they cannot ever recover from the humiliation or the hurt. Many have taken their own lives.

Bullies are slowly being held accountable for their actions, charged as criminals. Unfortunately, it has only been after many reported deaths that our society has said, "No more." We are finally coming together and forming a united front against bullying, which starts with young children as teasing or hurtful words. Dr. B. Beale of Child and Adolescent Behavioral Health in Canton, Ohio, told the story of how her thirteen-year-old son and his friends witnessed several bullying incidents at their school. They were able to intervene, challenge the bully, and protect the target, but only with the support and encouragement of both their parents and teachers. She said that, if bystanders can be mobilized to interrupt or simply report bullying, they feel empowered and proud, changing the emotional tone from fear and anxiety.

## Government Action

The Ohio Statute on Bullying in the Schools, effective in March 2007, requires local boards of education to establish anti-bullying policies and procedures, including protection strategies and disciplinary procedures. Other states around the country have put similar policies into effect. School districts are encouraged to form bullying prevention task forces and provide training around these issues. Unfortunately, many school administrators feel overwhelmed and don't know where to start. Others

---

52 *Touchpoints: The Essential Reference*, 439.

are confused, reporting they already have behavioral standards and wonder why they need to create new policies or procedures. In truth, there is no easy answer and no simple solution. Bullying is pervasive and dangerous with long-term, negative effects for both the targets and the bullies. One Ohio school district set up a hotline for students and families to call if they wanted to discuss or report bullying, and adults asking how to deal with their own bullying situations filled the lines. Simply establishing rules and consequences in our schools will never be enough. Everyone needs to acknowledge the problem and do his part to change our culture.

Multifaceted strategies to reduce bullying in schools are more likely to succeed than single component programs. System-wide training, monitoring, and assessment; classroom focus on reinforcing rules and building social-emotional skills; and specific interventions beyond punishment for students who are targets or perpetrators of bullying are all needed simultaneously. Schools must have clear definitions and procedures in place with firm consequences that are consistently implemented. Regrettably, adults are only minimally aware of the bullying incidents that occur. Most students do not report being bullied for two simple reasons: the belief that nothing will be done to help or protect them and the fear that the bullying will escalate.

## What Can I Do?

When it comes to controlling bullying, parents can help. Talk to your kids about bullying, not just once, but every week, and really listen to what they have to say. Ask probing questions about behaviors and feelings. It may take some repetition to help them understand that you really do want to know what concerns them. If they share that they have been targeted, offer support, and assure them that no one deserves to be bullied. Provide encouragement, and assist with reporting. While many bullying incidents happen without adult observation, most occur with other students nearby. A newer strategy being examined is to transform the bystanders into rescuers. A rescuer observes, steps in, and stands up to a bully, drawing attention to his actions and support for the target.

## Week of Awareness

When I taught disabled high school students in New Jersey, we provided a one-week requirement each fall to integrate our lessons with specific information with the goal of increasing an awareness of bullying and nonviolence. The objective was to promote increased acts of kindness throughout the school. One week out of each school year was dedicated to eliminating a life-threatening behavior. I watched the effectiveness, year after year, as I had a part in the many success stories. Parents can initiate an act of kindness jar in their home, rewarding their child with a stone or marble in the jar each time their child is thoughtful or kind. Sharing, offering help, or providing a compliment rather than a sarcastic remark are all acts of kindness that improve overall behavior, eventually diminishing teasing and bully behavior. When the jar is full, a fun family event can be planned in appreciation of all those thoughtful gestures. Teaching children how to be kind and rewarding them for that behavior with consistent, simple recognition is the scaffolding for kind, thoughtful behavior.

## Online Assistance

The following websites provide valuable information for parents, teachers, and children to learn more about and end bullying. We have many resources available to us. It's time to utilize them.

- **http://www.stopcyberbullying.org/why_do_kids_cyberbully_each_other.html:** Cyberbullying and how to stop it
- **www.webmd.com/parenting:** How to discourage attacks
- **www.parentfurther.com:** Ways to empower your child against bullies
- **http://www.lifescript.com/quizzes/parenting/is_your_child_a_bully.aspx:** How to determine if your child is a bully
- **http://www.parentsconnect.com/parenting-your-kids/parenting-kids/bullying/bullying_kids_protection.html:** How to help your child deal with a bully
- **www.thebullyactionguide.com:** Important information for parents
- **http://kidshealth.org/kid/feeling/emotion/bullies.html:** A PBS place for kids to talk about their bully experiences
- **www.stopbullyingnow.hrsa.gov:** How to stop bullying at school and encourage better interactions among students.
- **www.peacebuilders.com:** How to increase positive interactions

- **http://www.c-span.org/Events/Department-of-Educations-Bullying-Prevention-Summit/10737418459/:** Department of Education strategies to end bullying

- **www.antibullying.net:** Strategies to eliminate bullying in school.

- **www.stompOutBullying.org:** How to end bullying

- **http://abcnews.go.com/2020/TheLaw/school-bullying-epidemic-turning-deadly/story?id=11880841#.T5xXC7Py_P4:** Information on "Bullied to Death" from 20/20, an ABC news show

# Dear Diana

*A Ballet Bully*

Dear Diana, My four-year-old daughter attends a ballet class with other girls her age. One of her classmates is rude and intimidating and on the edge of being a bully. When the girls are told to line up, she runs and pushes all the others to get to the front of the line. When the girls are told to change shoes from ballet to tap, she tosses other girls' belongings to the side to find hers. We moms are in and out throughout the lessons, able to observe or provide help with changing. The mother of this girl has watched as her daughter has pushed others aside and done nothing. Other mothers have talked about what we should do because our girls don't want to be near her, for fear of being run over or having something mean said to them. I have never heard her say anything mean, but it is our girls' perception that she is intimidating since she seems to have no boundaries. My daughter has started to say that she doesn't want to go to ballet class anymore because of that one girl. What would you do? Thanks, Ballerina Mom

Dear Ballerina Mom, My heart actually goes out to the little girl who is pushing others because she has not been taught to wait patiently or walk carefully through a crowd. She has not been taught to think of others first or think of others at all. She is old enough to learn those skills and become aware of the impact she has on others. She will be the one to lose friends, as you have pointed out. She will be the one who is excluded from parties and playdates because neither the moms nor the other children want to be with her.

Children display behaviors they see at home, so perhaps older siblings or neighborhood friends are teaching her by pushing her out of the way with no one to stop or correct them or defend her. I can think of three reasons why her mom may not be stepping in. She may not know what to do about it when she sees it, she may not see it as problem behavior, or she truly may not see it when it happens. Neither blame nor judgment will help this little girl to learn, so the best thing to do is to come up with a positive game plan that will not offend the mom or intimidate the little girl. Otherwise, it will be a shame when this little girl will eventually become ostracized. She desperately needs to be taught manners and social skills, or she will, as you have said, be thought of as a bully or rude, and parents will not want their daughters to play with her. It could be a life-changing gift for you to gently help her learn some basics, which will help the other girls be more comfortable with her.

Approach the ballet teacher to make her aware of what is happening in her class. She will not want to see her ballerinas drop out, so I think she would be helpful in directing the girls to line up according to height, age, or alphabetically. She can also address personal space, which they should already be learning about as a basic ballet skill. When the girls are changing, perhaps you can sit in between her and your daughter to help them both learn to touch only what belongs to them. Verbally identify what you see as a method of teaching. Talk to both girls in a gentle voice with compliments of how careful they are not to toss around other people's belongings. Recognize and verbalize a new, positive behavior when you see her walk without pushing. Give her a wink and a touch when you are near her, and tell her it is great that she walks across the room or you have noticed she is finding her belongings with her eyes instead of her hands as she used to do when she tossed everyone's things.

This little ballerina bully may have absolutely no awareness that she has disrupted or frightened her classmates. Teaching outside of the event is effective, especially when you can praise any part of a new or desirable behavior. Tell her mom that you have noticed how careful her daughter is trying to be when they line up. Chances are that her mom has some awareness of how well liked her daughter is or isn't. Perhaps all of you could stop for ice cream after a class. When others feel included and connected, they often become more thoughtful.

# 13

# Traditions

## Introduction: Memories That Last a Lifetime

When we think of traditions, many of us immediately think of holidays. However, traditions can be initiated, created, and introduced into your home at any time of year. Traditions are simply the reoccurrence of a same behavior, an action, an event, or a celebration. Many families have birthday traditions, and most have seasonal traditions. You may develop a warm, comforting feeling as you reminisce over your own family's traditions that you enjoyed when you were young. Traditions bring a sense of security through sameness, especially for young children. Traditions unite a family. Traditions set one family apart from another since traditional activities are as different as each family. Traditions ignite uniqueness and help children to feel special with strong, loyal, familial bonds. Traditions can engage everyone and become the cement for your family.

Think of any traditions you have surrounding holidays on Fourth of July, Christmas, Chanukah, Valentine's Day, St. Patrick's Day, Memorial Day, Labor Day, and, of course, birthdays. Chances are you have more traditions in place than you realized. Take a minute to think of the memories you have already created for your children with those traditions. Now, think of new traditions you might initiate with your family, such as always serving a big pancake breakfast on the first day back to school after the long summer vacation, Friday night pizza with family game board night, starting each Sunday morning with cinnamon rolls, tucking your child in each night as you tell him all the reasons he is so special, going for a family walk with flashlights on the first night of summer, or heading outside with a cup of hot chocolate to catch snowflakes on your tongue at the first snowfall. It is so heartwarming to hear a child say, "Well, in my house, we have a birthday tradition where my mom ties balloons to the birthday person's bedpost and then hangs streamers all over the kitchen and makes a special birthday breakfast!" The excitement from such a simple action can produce wonderful family bonding with memories that will last a lifetime and may even be handed down to your children's family. Just before this publication, I was fortunate enough to receive a beautiful card from my twenty-three-year-old daughter, thanking me for creating so many special celebrations and magical moments that she holds in her memory. This chapter offers multiple articles on a variety of family traditions and the impact that those traditions continue to have throughout the years.

## Birthdays and Holiday Birthdays

I am often asked my thoughts about the importance of birthdays, the need for elaborate parties, or how to best celebrate children who were born around a holiday. The tradition of birthday celebrations began hundreds of years ago in Europe, where it was thought that evil spirits were attracted to a person on his day of birth. To ensure his safety and good health, friends and family gathered to protect and celebrate the birthday person. Royalty sent announcements and invitations to fill their palace with guests, protecting themselves from harm. And it is thought that, as commoners carried forth the tradition in their small homes to be celebrated or protected on their birthdays, they began to wear crowns, just as the royalty did, giving us the tradition of the birthday crown.[53] Various cultures and religions celebrate birthdays in different ways, and some don't do anything at all. Many families have special birthday traditions, which each family member treasures. There are endless, wonderful family birthday traditions online to inspire a birthday celebration of any sort.

## Our Traditions

I believe that a birthday is a once-a-year opportunity to pay special tribute to and provide extra recognition for all that person is and has done. As I was growing up, my dad hand-painted our birthday cards, which I still hold and treasure. While raising my children, on the eve of birthdays,

---

53 www.birthdaycelebrations.net/traditions.htm

after the birthday child went to bed, I blew up bunches of large balloons tied to colorful ribbons and quietly hung them to bedposts, dresser drawer knobs, lamps, and bedroom door handle. I worked my way downstairs, hanging balloons onto the chandelier, the breakfast "birthday chair," and the mailbox outside. The balloons alone made my birthday child feel special and celebrated with neighbors noticing the balloons outside and wishing him well on his way to school.

When I was a child, I received special hand-painted birthday cards from my father, and my grandmother wrote her own poems or rhymes each year, sealing every birthday card with a lipstick kiss. Those traditions carried on to my children with a hand-painted card from their grandfather and a poem sealed with a kiss from their great-grandmother. My children always knew when a card arrived from Great-grandmother GiGi. In our home, birthdays started with a special breakfast of waffles with whipped cream and ended with the birthday person's favorite dinner in the dining room.

Thanksgiving is a busy time of year for so many. It includes a gathering of loved ones, the thoughtful recognition of gratitude, the excitement of family traditions, and fabulous comfort food. And then begins the start of the holiday season! A child's birthday can easily become overlooked or minimized when it falls around a holiday.

My first child, Benjamin, was born on Thanksgiving morning twenty-nine years ago. I had so much to be thankful for that day. As he grew up, I built birthday parties around the season, inviting busy friends and family to celebrate his birthday, which fell on Thanksgiving or a day or two before or after. Although everyone was busy, a themed hayride through farm fields, an ice skating party with hot chocolate and doughnuts, and a gingerbread house building contest are among the parties we all remember with great fondness. They brought everyone together in laughter and love.

My mom's birthday is December 16, and although so many friends and family are thoroughly wrapped up with holiday preparations, parties, and shopping, we spend the day together, reminiscing and celebrating her amazing life. Sometimes, the importance of a birthday is lost when it is squeezed into a family holiday celebration. Therefore, some families choose to celebrate half-birthdays for just that reason. A December birthday celebrated in June can bring on a whole new dimension for a winter baby, providing great weather for an outdoor-themed party. Of course, every family celebrates in its own way, some big and some with discretion, but I have never met anyone who didn't appreciate a little extra attention or recognition, making him feel loved and appreciated on his special day. To my son Ben, my mom, and all those born around a celebrated holiday, happy birthday!

## Thanksgiving Traditions

The holiday season is like no other, where families gather from around the country and some from around the world, to give thanks, to celebrate, to prepare meals, and to break bread together. It is the time of year when we go back to our roots, returning to the home where we grew up or reminiscing in our hearts as we return through our memories, gathering together with family. This is the season where leaves are piled high, the air is crisp, fireplaces crackle, and children begin to dream of snowflakes, sleigh rides, and twinkling, colored lights.

Including children in holiday preparations will help them to feel connected, increase their feeling of self-worth, and provide them with a wonderful foundation for your family's heritage and traditions. Inviting them to participate with special table decorations or meal preparation will help them become invested in the day, sparking their interest to learn and do more. We often get so busy and feel that little hands make for more work. However, including children with preparations can be easier than trying to keep them busy and out of trouble.

These simple projects can ignite new traditions with childhood memories to last a lifetime:

- Make colorful Thanksgiving place mats for each guest. Place your child's painted thumbprint all over a page of construction paper for a field of turkeys. Use his thumbprint as the turkey's body, adding two legs, colorful feather squiggles, and a triangle beak with a gobble. Cover each place mat with clear contact paper, and send them home with each guest after dinner.

- A scooped-out pumpkin can become a magnificent centerpiece. Use garden flowers, leaves, or berries, which your child can collect. Use toothpicks and wooden skewers to secure your foliage.

- Pilgrim ships made from halved walnut shells will provide a bit of history. They are easily made with the halved shells as the base for each boat, a toothpick stuck in some clay for the mast, and a small, triangular piece of paper for the sail.

- Make table place cards. Trace your child's hand, and have him color the fingers to become the feathers. Draw a simple beak and waddle added on the thumb, the turkey's head. Each guest will enjoy his handmade turkey place card.

I recall our holiday aprons were carefully unwrapped from tissue paper from storage. I was filled with delight, knowing I would have an opportunity to help bake pies and roll cinnamon in leftover pastry dough. My sister and I were also permitted to unwrap the small glass turkey salt and pepper shakers, as well as pilgrim candles, which we carefully placed on the table. Being included in the food preparation for these special meals meant we were given special time to learn how to roll out a pie crust or carefully slice apples for the pies with a butter knife, of course. My sister and I reveled in the delight of our special children's table, which was always as beautifully decorated as the main table, making us feel as important as our guests.

My mom always opened our home and invited others who didn't have a place to go. At the time, I wondered why we couldn't just have our own family for dinner, but each year, we learned about new cultures and traditions, and our family's circle of friends grew larger. I now realize what my mom was giving to others, and she taught us how to give.

This holiday season, provide each guest or family member with oversized index card to note and preserve his traditions, recipes, and family stories. Everyone's family is his treasure chest. Each guest can note old and new experiences, old and new war stories, remembrances of traditional roles no longer carried out, and favorite recipes no longer prepared throughout the day. Everyone can provide something from his memory to be preserved forever and given to your child. Talk about grandparents, great-grandparents, cousins, and extended family. Find out who was a war hero. Who made it to college back in the day of a one-room schoolhouse? Who worked on the railroad, helping to build America? These cards can be archived for a time when your child is more capable of learning and joining in, as new stories are told and old ones are retold.

## The Gift of Tradition

Family traditions provide lifelong memories. Those who recall and share their family traditions often do so with a warm, loving smile. Everyone who participates in a tradition becomes a part of the memory. A family united in tradition is one that shares joy and communicates love through their custom. Although traditions occur throughout the year, it seems that, with the snap of the cold weather and the lighting of lights, many customs and practices flood into memory.

Store-bought gingerbread men cookies can be personalized and decorated with mittens and smiles to deliver to a nursing home. Candy canes transformed into reindeer with pipe cleaners for antlers, googly eyes glued on, and a red puffball for a nose can be offered to neighbors. Provide children with an opportunity to earn a few dollars so they can purchase inexpensive gifts. Thoughtfully choosing or making a special gift for family, neighbors, or friends will build self-pride and ignite good feelings from gift giving.

Making a gingerbread house is a fun tradition at any time during the winter season. The foundation of each house is a small, pint-sized milk carton, covered with white frosting as the glue and layered with graham crackers. Candies cover the house and can be glued on with white snowy frosting so your child can choose a treat from his gingerbread house to eat each day.

One of our many family Christmas traditions was that my grandmother, my mom, and I each bought my three my children a beautiful ornament, representing something each had a passion for, someplace we had visited, or something each had accomplished that year. Names and dates were always written on the ornament, and now each of my three children has twenty-plus years of ornaments for his own family tree. We open them up, year after year, with anticipation and time to reminisce.

Special collections of village houses and nutcrackers that are only brought out once a year can bring joy and excitement, as children learn to handle each with care and wonder. In our home, Christmas morning was not complete without a traditional brunch of Belgian waffles topped with whipped cream and strawberries, cinnamon rolls, eggs, fruit, and sparkling cider. It always completed our special Christmas breakfast, and it is a tradition we continue to enjoy. My neighbor said she remembers her mom hanging little silver bells all around the lower branches of their tree, so she could tell when the children were going near to sneak a peek at the gifts. Little silver bells still bring back wonderful childhood memories for her.

Growing up, my mom initiated some traditions that I recall with great fondness. Although we gave gifts of garden bouquets and baked goods to neighbors all year long, at Christmastime, we prepared pomander balls, pushing hundreds of cloves into an orange and then wrapping them in netting and ribbon to fill the house with a warm, wintery scent. In addition to leaving Santa some cookies and milk, we peeled carrots and strung bells on ribbons for Santa's reindeer. After Christmas, my mom kept us busy as we cut out pictures from holiday cards, punched holes, and tied ribbons to use for next year's gift tags. We were recycling before our time! And a very fond memory is of each New Year's Eve when my mom baked a round cake and designed it with the face of a clock at midnight. A basket of blowers and party hats helped us feel important, and although we were too young to stay up for the New Year, my mom included us in that special occasion.

Children learn so much by being a part of family traditions. They come to understand the beauty of sharing and giving. The sparkle in their eyes grows brighter each year from giving, not always from getting. Spending time as a family, making gifts to give, thinking of others, decorating, singing, and visiting those without family are the scaffolding that will help to build who they will become. During this beautiful season, think of giving everyone in your family the gift of a tradition.

## Dear Diana

*Santa Claus*

Dear Diana, What should I say or do to handle my five-year-old who yelled at Santa? After he gave her a toy, she realized he had a fake beard and hair, and she demanded the real Santa! I feel like she's too young for me to tell her the truth. I want her to continue to believe in Santa, as she has an older, seven-year-old sister who still believes. Mom of Two Girls

Dear Mom of Two, Many parents question how to handle the magic of the season when a child starts to doubt Santa. In this case, while you are continuing to nurture the fantasy, you can tell your daughter that Santa has lots and lots of helpers who talk with all the children and then report back to Santa at the North Pole. The next issue to address with your daughter is that she may never be rude and she may not yell at others. Where do you think she learned that from? Someone in her life has modeled that behavior, making her feel comfortable enough to behave in that manner. Teach her to always be respectful, no matter what. She is learning from you, so model that for her.

*Three Wise Things*

To help remediate her behavior, your daughter needs to understand three things very clearly.

- She needs to understand and verbalize what she did (sit on Santa's lap, accept a gift, and then get angry and yell at Santa).

- She needs to understand and verbalize which part was unacceptable and what she could have done differently when she became upset.

- She needs to take responsibility in some way for her unacceptable behavior. You can take the toy away (which Santa's helper gave her) and allow to her to earn it back with polite behavior. Provide a time frame that is appropriate for her age. For instance, tell her that, if she displays polite manners for the next two days, she may earn it back.

Your daughter can also write a letter to Santa, apologizing to his helper for yelling at him. That action will help her understand what she did wrong. It will help her to take responsibility through her apology as well as further instill her belief in Santa, which is what you wanted.

## Enjoy the Magic

This can be a controversial subject for many because, on one hand, parents provide their child with a wonderful, magical fantasy, while on the other, they provide information that is not truthful. Some children and families lose the meaning of the holiday, whether it is religious or not because they are focused more on the presents rather than the true gifts.

I recall being a young girl and going to the bakery at Easter. The baker said he was giving iced bunny cookies to all the children who believed in the Easter Bunny. When I said I believed, he laughed but then apologized for ruining my fairy tale. When we left the bakery without an iced cookie, I asked my mom if that meant there was not a tooth fairy, Santa, leprechauns, or other magical beings. She said we always carry the magic in our hearts and can find it at any time. She reminded me of the time our family drove to the North Pole (in upstate New York) to visit Santa's workshop with elves busily making toys and eight reindeer in the barn. The snow was deep, the air was snapping cold, and the magic was everywhere. She also reminded me of the many years my sister and I watched in awe as the Easter Bunny filled our baskets. Little did we know that our dad had painted a stuffed animal rabbit with florescent paint and tied wires to it from the chandelier with a pull string into the kitchen so it would hop from basket to basket in the dark dining room. My mom asked that I tell her about my memories, and as I did, the warmth, love, and celebration of each occasion came swelling back and did fill my heart, just as she said it would. Enjoy the magic of each season. Never overlook even the smallest opportunity to teach your child the values you want her to live by.

## Disclaimer

Always contact your pediatrician with any medical, developmental, or behavioral concerns, as guidelines are available for typical development. For the best outcome, a mental health provider should see those children who display clinically recognized criteria for depression or oppositional behavior. However, in any situation, your approach to parenting will always have a direct impact on your child's success.

## Special Thanks

With appreciation, I thank Jeff Gauger, executive editor of *The Repository*, owned by Gatehouse Media. He believed in me by believing that parents would benefit from a weekly column solely dedicated to their parenting concerns. With gratitude, I thank Gary Brown and Melissa Griffy, who thoughtfully edited my lengthy subject matter into newspaper-friendly information of seven hundred words or fewer. *Family Matters* is a syndicated column read from coast to coast, and a weekly blog can be found at www.yourperfectchild.com.

# References

## Books

Allen, K. Eileen, and Lynn R. Marotz, PhD, RN. *Developmental Profiles: Pre-Birth through Eight.* Canada: Delmar Publishers, 1999.

Borba, Michele, EdD. *The Big Book of Parenting Solutions.* San Francisco: Jossey Bass, 2009.

Brazelton, T. Berry, MD. *Touchpoints: The Essential Reference.* Reading, Mass.: Perseus Books, 1992.

Ferber, Richard, MD. *Solve Your Child's Sleep Problems.* New York: Simon and Schuster, 1985.

Fogel, Alan. *Infancy: Infant, Family, and Society.* St. Paul, Minn.: West Publishing Company, 1991.

Foxman, Paul, PhD. *The Worried Child.* Alameda, Calif.: Hunter House Publications, 2004.

Kurchinka, Mary Sheedy. *Raising Your Spirited Child.* New York: HarperCollins Publisher, 1991.

Miller, Karen. *Ages and Stages.* Telshare Publishing Company, 1985.

Severe, Sal, PhD. *How to Behave So Your Child Will Too!* New York: Penguin Books, 2003.

Shure, Myrna B., PhD. *Thinking Parent, Thinking Child.* New York: McGraw Hill, 2005.

Webster-Stratton, Carolyn, PhD. *The Incredible Years*. Washington: Incredible Years, 2005.

Zigler, Edward F., Matia Finn-Stevenson, and Nancy W. Hale. *The First Three Years and Beyond*. New Haven, Conn.: Yale University Press, 2002.

## Correspondence

Thomas Jefferson's letter to Peter Carr, Paris, August 19, 1785.

## Videos

Rob Reiner, director, *I am Your Child. The First Years Last Forever*. 1997.

## Websites

www.babyzone.com/toddler/article/daylight-savings-time

http://www.birthdaycelebrations.net/traditions.htm

www.brainyquote.com/quotes/quotes/a/alfredlord153702.htm

www.bullyfree.com/free-resources/facts-about-bullying

http://bungelab.blogspot.com  Post: Tues. Feb 2, 2010

www.murphys-laws.com/murphy/murphy-toddler.htm